PENGUIN BOOKS
Life After Death

Life After Death

Messages of Love from the Other Side

SALLY MORGAN

PENGUIN BOOKS

PENGUIN BOOKS

Published by the Penguin Group
Penguin Books Ltd, 80 Strand, London WC2R ORL, England
Penguin Group (USA) Inc., 375 Hudson Street, New York, New York 10014, USA
Penguin Group (Canada), 90 Eglinton Avenue East, Suite 700, Toronto, Ontario, Canada M4P 2Y3
(a division of Pearson Penguin Canada Inc.)
Penguin Ireland, 25 St Stephen's Green, Dublin 2, Ireland
(a division of Penguin Books Ltd)
Penguin Group (Australia), 250 Camberwell Road,
Camberwell, Victoria 3124, Australia (a division of Pearson Australia Group Pty Ltd)
Penguin Books India Pvt Ltd, 11 Community Centre,
Panchsheel Park, New Delhi – 110 017, India
Penguin Group (NZ), 67 Apollo Drive, Rosedale, Auckland 0632, New Zealand
(a division of Pearson New Zealand Ltd)
Penguin Books (South Africa) (Pty) Ltd, 24 Sturdee Avenue,
Rosebank, Johannesburg 2196, South Africa

Penguin Books Ltd, Registered Offices: 80 Strand, London WC2R ORL, England

www.penguin.com

First published 2011
7

Copyright © Sally Morgan and Nick Harding, 2011
All rights reserved

The moral right of the authors has been asserted

Set in 12.5/14.75pt Garamond MT Std
Typeset by Jouve (UK), Milton Keynes
Printed in England by Clays Ltd, St Ives plc

ISBN: 978-0-241-95282-5

www.greenpenguin.co.uk

MIX
Paper from
responsible sources
FSC www.fsc.org   FSC™ C018179

Penguin Books is committed to a sustainable
future for our business, our readers and our
planet. This book is made from paper certified
by the Forest Stewardship Council.

In memory of Jean Ibottson, who passed in 2010

PART ONE

The Power of Psychic Energy

Voices in My Head

Backstage, waiting in the wings, the noise level rises in my ears. I can't pick out individual voices, but the sound of the audience is like the sea, building and retreating in swells and ebbs like the waves of a distant ocean. It is made of hundreds of individual parts; voices and laughter flowing together to form a singular body. It sings in tandem with another more primal force, invisible to the human ear but perceptible in my mind. This is the hum of energy that builds up, in and around me as I wait to open the gates, swelling from a place so sacred and so divine that it transcends rational explanation. This is the sound of the dead and it harmonizes with the physical sound to form a symphony. I step from one foot to the other, holding my assistant Julie's hand, focusing on the two elements; the audience and the energy that issues forth from spirit, both expectant and both waiting to be united.

I stand in the shadows, waiting. No one in the crowd can see me and I can't see them. Little bits of tape stuck to the floor mark out the places where I am invisible, the places I can stand out of sight, ready to venture into the spotlight. I don't want them to see me before it's time. It's all part of the show. But spirit knows I am here and it knows what I am here to do. And it's becoming excitable.

It's always black back there in the nooks and crannies of the UK's theatres. You could be in any theatre in any city and the set-up would be the same; dark curtains, dark flooring, dark walls. A blank canvas ready to be painted.

The montage on the screen at the back of the stage begins and the audience chatter subsides. I'm prickling like a ball of static electricity. As the introduction music booms from the speakers, individual names and images are beginning to pop into my head. The door to spirit is opening. A rose, a fire, the name Rex, keys falling from a window, John, Annie, Vera, a dog, the twisted wreckage of a car – images, sounds and voices flash into my subconscious.

'Not yet,' I whisper to them. 'Just a few more seconds.'

I'm not sure how I do it but somewhere, somehow I put up a barrier. The energy becomes a hum again, like the white noise between radio stations, only soothing, like notes on a piano synthesized and elongated. A beautiful noise, unworldly and strange, yet familiar and comforting at the same time.

As the introduction finishes playing on stage, Julie gives my hand a squeeze.

'It's showtime!' She smiles.

I step forward from the shadows, bathed in stage light. It is time for me to make my introductions; it is time for the living and the dead to meet.

The cheers and applause never fail to humble me. All these people have parted with their hard-earned cash to come and see me. No matter how many shows I do – and I have done plenty – believe me, I will always feel grateful and lucky when I enter from stage left and take those first steps to meet the audience. Somewhere, deep in my mind, something clicks. The floodgates are opened. The energy flows in.

Before the stage shows I could never quite understand why the Rolling Stones still toured. Why would anyone that age and with an eye-watering bank balance still be willing to hit the road and travel the world staging ever more spectacular gigs? But now I understand. They don't do it for the money, nor for the fame or the recognition. They do it for that unique feeling you get when you first walk from the wings on to the stage in front of an audience. It is one of the most exhilarating feelings anyone is likely to experience.

As the clapping subsides, it's time to get to work.

The energy swirls around me like a cloud of twinkling stars and the stars begin to crystallize into words and shapes and images. They swim around me and through me. There are people on stage with me now. To the audience they are invisible; they are not formed of flesh and blood. They abandoned their physical vessels long ago, but they are there and they want to be known. They are the dead; they are the souls of the departed. Some are serene and beautiful; others bear the marks of horrible tragedy, injury and illness; there are the young and the old, men and women, sometimes even cats and dogs. It can be a strange carnival that materializes with me.

They show me their wounds, they tell me their hopes and fears, they whisper their secrets and show me snatches of their lives. Some wait anxiously, quietly, looking out into the audience; others are more vocal: they jump up and down pointing, laughing, shouting. They tell me things, they jostle and call names. They drift off and return. Sometimes it can be like looking after a class of unruly schoolchildren. One thing I can say for sure is that, in the afterlife, we lose our British ability to queue! They butt in and try to hijack each other.

I'm in the middle, all five foot of me, trying to referee this jamboree of the dead. They are pure energy: psychic energy, spiritual energy. They form a cloud, a nebula that spins around the room, filling the empty space and spitting out names and information. It is a process both beautiful and awe-inspiring, and sometimes overpowering. The energy is the key to it all. I am beginning to understand this. It is the force that sits inside us all, and it is what ensures we live on after we die. It is as old as time; it is our soul. Each and every one of us, every living being, carries its own measure of that energy.

Now, as I allow the energy in, the names and images are filling me up. I start to concentrate on individual strands. I start to convulse.

'I'm shaking,' I tell the audience. 'I'm here with a man and I feel like I'm shaking. I can't control myself.' The spirit tells me his passing was recent. 'He died within the last month,' I explain. Then the name Peter appears in my head. I am directed towards the left-hand side of the stalls.

'Who is Peter?' I throw the question out to the part of the audience I feel drawn to. A hand shoots up. 'Stand up, love,' I tell the woman, who now has a microphone in her hand. 'I have a Peter, he can't control his arms and he is confused. His passing was very recent, wasn't it?'

She nods her head. 'Three weeks ago,' she says.

More images and words flash into my head. I'm looking at the body of a man, laid out on a hospital bed. He is dead, covered in a crisp white sheet. His eyes are closed, there is the ghost of a smile on his lips. He is at peace.

Then I'm above the body and I see the back of a woman's head leaning over him, sobbing. 'I'm sorry, Dad,' she is saying. 'I'm sorry I wasn't there.' A flashback. I see the man dying, alone (later, nurses surround him), and by the side of his bed there is a photo of a young woman and two small children. She is the same woman who came to his body after he passed.

'Who is Ben?' I ask as another name materializes in my mind.

'My son,' answers the woman.

'. . . and Michael?'

'My other son.'

I feel a glow and a warm smile from the spirit.

'He loved them so much,' I tell the woman who I now know is Peter's daughter.

I see the children on a climbing frame in a sun-dappled garden. Their laughter drifts through the air, dancing on the breeze, rippling like a heat haze.

'He watches them in the garden,' I tell her. 'He loves seeing them play together. He is so proud of them.'

'He always sat on the bench and watched them,' she smiles through tears of longing. 'Is he OK? Did he suffer?'

'He's fine,' I tell her. 'He's in Heaven. He's in a wonderful place, surrounded by love.'

Then, as clear as day, Peter tells me what he has come all this way to say: 'She mustn't feel guilty. I see her crying and she doesn't have to. I was not alone. My mum came for me.'

'You've been living with guilt, haven't you?' I ask the woman.

She nods.

'His mum was there with him, you know. She came and got him. She took him. No one goes alone. There is always someone waiting on the other side. You don't have to be upset that you weren't there. It isn't your fault, and he wants you to know that and to leave the guilt behind.'

Tearfully she nods her head.

'And who is Vera?' I ask. 'There's a Vera with him, she's tugging at my sleeve.'

I can feel urgent yanks on my arm as an old lady dressed in a checked pinny swoops into my field of concentration along with Peter. Her name is placed firmly in my mind, the way someone might slam a mug down on a kitchen surface. It's as if she has pushed her name to the front of my brain. Then another name arrives, Vinnie, and with it the feeling I am falling from a window.

'Some of the things that come out of my mouth sound mad,' I tell the woman, 'but over the years I have learned to trust them. I'm old enough not to worry about looking silly. I have a Vera here and she's showing me a roof in an old house. She's saying, "It's ruined, it's ruined." And she's with someone, a man. I think his name is Vinnie. When I look at this person I feel I am falling from a window. It's a first-floor window over a door. Does any of that make any sense to you at all?'

I've learned by now that what I do is not an exact science. There needs to be a little trust involved on all sides, because the messages that come through are often garbled.

The lady shakes her head. She doesn't know anyone named Vera or Vinnie.

Then, two rows behind her, a hand reluctantly rises. A smartly dressed elderly gentleman with snowy-white hair gets to his feet and is passed the microphone. By now, Vera is shouting excitedly in my mind.

'Vera's asking if you got the roof sorted?' I say to him. 'Does that mean anything to you?'

He nods, a soft smile playing on his lips.

A prickling sensation shoots through my chest and down my arm. This has happened to me so many times I automatically know what it means.

'It was her heart, wasn't it?' I ask. 'She was such a fighter, she held on as long as she could, but in the end her heart just gave up. It was her time.'

He confirms that Vera was his wife. She had died three years before, of a heart attack, and only last week he had had to call pest control to the home he had lived in with Vera for twenty-five years because squirrels had nested in the roof.

But there is still an unchecked box.

'I still have Vinnie,' I tell the man. 'Is there someone in your family in spirit called Vinnie?'

He racks his brain and shakes his head.

Then another random thought materializes in my mind.

'A Roma,' I say. But it comes out in a strange accent. I laugh, and the audience laughs with me.

The man is still standing up ten rows in front of me and by now he looks utterly baffled.

'Ever been to Rome maybe?' I try. I know that somewhere, somehow, this message means something to someone. Often I will give details that have been given to me and, initially, they mean nothing. They might be dates or names or places or random snatches of information. The receiver (the person receiving the message) will shrug and shake their head. In 99 per cent of readings, however, they'll go away and, a day, a week or even a year later, suddenly, *ping*, that seemingly unconnected detail will suddenly make sense. It might seem random at times but, trust me, there's nothing random about the messages spirit passes on.

In the shadows, at the back of the circle, I can just about make out a hand. The cameraman on stage next to me spots it and moves the camera on its tripod to focus in on the man who is waving from the last row up in the gods.

I turn to look at the screen behind me, where his face swims into focus.

'Hello, love,' I say.

He's a tall, dark man, not more than thirty years old. He is clean-shaven and his shoulder-length black hair falls in curls over his forehead. His eyes twinkle and there's a nervous smile on his lips.

'Hello,' he answers in an accent as thick as treacle.

The babble that has been going on around me calms, the voices respectfully hush to whispers. It's hard to explain with words, but I feel a line of energy connect from me to the young man. At first the energy beam is wide and hazy, but it gradually brightens and contracts into a brilliant-white laser beam of light, like sunlight when it's focused through a magnifying glass. The beam aims straight for the man's chest. He's pinned on it, like a butterfly in a museum display case. A connection is made.

With his sultry accent ringing in my ears, I ask confidently: 'I keep hearing the words "a Roma". Are you from Italy?'

'No,' he replies. 'I am Russian.' The audience chuckles.

But the connection from the spirit world that now links me to this man is so strong I know he is meant to be here and I know this message is for him. I feel two people on stage with me, I can feel their energy pulsing in expectation. I concentrate on that energy and it becomes clearer; it shows me the detail I need. I see the two people now. There is an old woman, grey and wrinkled, dressed in a simple green dress with a lace headscarf. She has hollowed cheeks and several of her teeth are missing. She looks old and tired; she had a hard life, I sense. With her is a young man. He's wearing jeans, a white T-shirt and a leather jacket. His eyes are fierce, defiant. He stands upright with a straight back and a strong chest. Connected to him I sense injustice: he should not be there on the other side. The words 'a Roma' and 'Vinnie' are still ringing through my head and I feel as though I am falling. I see that first-floor window again.

I tell the man in the audience exactly what is in my head.

'Does any of this make sense to you?' I ask.

'Yes,' he nods. 'Roma is my brother. He was murdered. They have never caught the killer. We still do not know who did it.' The audience gasps.

The man then goes on to explain that the woman I have described is his mother. When she came to visit him, he would throw a key to her out of the window of his first-floor flat so she could let herself in. She died two years before, when she fell down a flight of stairs.

'But who is Vinnie?' I ask.

'That is my surname,' he answers. 'Vinychencko.'

The spirits glow with an iridescent love.

'They want you to know that they are in a wonderful, loving place and they are at peace. They are proud of you and they will be waiting for you.'

I pick up another energy: the spirit of another young man who died tragically. I am being shown a game of football.

'Did your brother play football?' I ask.

The man shakes his head. 'Was he thirty-two when he died, or is the number thirty-two important?'

He thinks and shakes his head again.

I feel my gaze being moved away from him, as if a pair of invisible hands is cupping my ears and moving my head to look across the balcony.

'It's not for you,' I tell him, and ask the audience to give him a round of applause.

I'm now being shown a football pitch and a team of players. Words are whispered in my head: 'It was so sudden, so sudden,' they repeat over and over. Then a name: Jack.

'I have a young man here,' I explain to the people in the area to which I now feel drawn. 'His passing was very sudden. No one expected it. There was no illness, he just keeled over one day and that was it.'

A girl in the audience a few seats from the Russian gentleman raises her hand. She's in her early twenties and wears a tight-fitting vest top. Her dyed blonde hair is cut in a bob and she has a gold chain around her neck with a dragonfly pendant attached to it.

'My boyfriend had a friend who died of Sudden Adult Death Syndrome while he was playing football. He was thirty-two.'

'I have him here,' I tell her. She's shaking. 'Who is Jack?'

'That's his son.'

A warning pops into my head.

'Jack needs to watch out for his shoulder,' I explain.

'There may be an injury. It won't be bad but he needs to make sure he sees a doctor just to get it checked out.'

She nods.

The messages continue. Each rolls into the next as the energy around me, the spirits that I am tuning into, hone in on each other's messages. They are like pieces of a jig-saw: they slot together piece by piece. As soon as one connection is made between a spirit and a receiver, I begin to pick up words and images from others in spirit with similar themes, or for people in the audience sitting near the person who is getting the message. It is like a form of psychic magnetism. Spirits are drawn to each other's ener-gies, like moths around a flame. They circle, waiting to swoop in.

This collective effect of mass energy that is generated when hundreds of spirits gather together is a different experience from what I had been used to in the years when I was building up my work as a medium through one-to-one readings at home. Back then it was just me and one other person sitting with me. I never got to experience the power of the combined energy created when a theatreful of people link with their departed loved ones. I never got to see the key to it all, to life after death. The key is the energy.

The Energy Connection

It begins with a soft hum, a gentle buzz in the back of my mind, like that of a single light bulb in an otherwise silent room. I can hear it in my head but it is not quite noise, more like a current of electricity. It is hard to describe because, frankly, I don't yet fully understand myself what goes on, and I've been experiencing it for nearly sixty years. The best way I can explain it is like this: have you ever sat in one of those fake electric chairs at a funfair where you hold the metal handles and a current slowly builds up along your arms? Well, it's like that, but it happens in my head. I sound mad already, don't I?

The build-up starts with individual currents humming in harmony with each other. Sometimes a part of the humming crystallizes into a thought or a sound and I hear a whisper, a word, usually a name.

Each individual strand of energy is a spirit; it is the soul of a departed being. Congregating together, they create the hum, that distant call from a place I still don't completely understand. It's the collective energy of spirit. It's the noise of the afterlife, the voices of hundreds of spirits murmuring through my thoughts, calling to me from across the divide, excited and sometimes urgent, hoping to get a message to someone in the audience at one of my live shows.

The process begins to happen when I'm sitting alone in the bowels of a theatre – any theatre, it doesn't matter, it's always the same. Spirits do not exist in the same realm as we do, so space and time have no meaning for them. I'll usually be putting on my make-up, doing my hair and changing into my stage outfit when it starts.

At every show I have a little ritual, and I didn't even realize I performed it until one of my stage crew pointed it out to me. I'll go to my dressing room and I'll hang my three garments for the evening in exactly the same way. The hangers will always point in the same direction and the outfits will always be in the same order: first-half stage outfit at the front, second-half stage outfit in the middle and book-signing outfit at the back. Then I'll carefully lay out my make-up in order: brushes to the side, eye make-up, lippy, foundation and powder all grouped together in sections on the counter in front of the mirror. I haven't got OCD, honestly! I think the ritual just helps me focus on the show. And as I go through the funny little routines of getting ready, the humming starts, because they know. They know soon I will open myself up to spirit and soon their loved ones will be coming through the front doors, taking their seats and praying for a sign, for a connection. They know something amazing is about to happen. They know the impossible is about to become possible. And they are getting excited, just as, hopefully, their loved ones are getting excited about the night ahead too.

I've been touring for several years now and, at first, when I sat there in my dressing room full of nerves and apprehension, crossing everything for a good night, the energy in my head seemed unusual and alien. I'd been used to it in a much clearer, defined way when I did one-to-one readings for clients in my home. The energy then was a distinct inner voice, like a thought process, but not my own and not one I was consciously controlling. It would pop words and images into my head, like a postman dropping mail through the letterbox. This otherworldly thought process ran parallel with my own and it would place such clear thoughts in my mind that I would see things, sometimes great, sweeping visions of men during wartime or a family surrounding a dying woman in a hospital ward, and other times a single object, such as a leather-bound book or a gold ring. I'd know automatically that whatever I was being 'given' in these thoughts was important to the person I was sitting with and I'd explain exactly and in as much detail as I could what I was seeing and hearing in my mind.

But in the theatres those single strands of energy congregate into a bustling mass. The locations and the scenery change, but the process that takes place within me remains the same. At first the energy building up is calming, a steady background noise, like waves or running water. As the auditorium begins to fill with people, the noise gets louder and louder. The theatre fills with life – and death.

Lately, this energy build-up is becoming more pronounced. It's as if word is spreading. Sometimes it's an effort to keep the energy at bay until the curtain goes up. You see, I've been practising, and practice makes perfect, as we all know. I've been touring for several years now, taking my psychic roadshow to larger and larger audiences, and I get the impression that spirit knows this. In the hour or so before the show starts, the energy can become a cacophony as spirits jostle for position, eager to connect with lost loves and family members, to give important messages or warnings, or sometimes just to say, 'Hello, I'm here, I love you.' Luckily, I'm able to have a degree of control over the whole process, otherwise they'd all come through in one big rush, like shoppers barging through the door at the New Year sales, and I'd probably fry my brain.

As I sit there, slicking on my lippy, some of those energy strands will form into clear thoughts, feelings, visions and voices. A name will suddenly jump out of my subconscious into the front of my mind. Often, it's so defined, I hear it as a sound in my head: 'Fred!' or 'Annie!' Sometimes, it's so clear and unexpected it makes me jump. You'd think I would be used to it by now, wouldn't you? But the truth is I never quite get used to dead people talking in my head, using me as a mouthpiece, especially when I'm not in work mode. If I see something or hear something from spirit when I'm not expecting it, I freak out, just like everybody else.

At other times, the thoughts present themselves as whispers: 'I'm here, Val. I miss you,' or 'Mummy, I'm OK, I'm with Gramps.' Sometimes they're funny, sometimes so tragically sad and desperate my heart aches and I cry with the person the message is meant for. Sometimes the spirits delivering the messages are shy; sometimes they are forceful. The one thing they all have in common is an air of expectation. I used to be daunted by it. I hate letting people down, living and dead, and when I have an audience of over a thousand people in front of me waiting for a message from a passed loved one and a cloud of expectant spirit energy surrounding me, I just never have enough time to pair every spirit up with every member of the audience. I know that I can't please everyone every night. I know that every night there will, sadly, be people who leave disappointed, for a number of reasons. They may have wanted a message but not have one, I may not have worked in the way they expected a medium to work (I think it's good to be unconventional, though – I don't get any complaints from spirit!), they may feel the whole process is too emotional for them. But I can't get too worried because, if I did, I wouldn't be able to do what I do. All I can hope for is that, each night when I step out on stage, I'll make some important connections, I'll reassure some people, I'll entertain others and I'll give everyone a sense of hope – hope that there is something when our loved ones and we ourselves pass away. Not much of a tick-list, is it?

Despite the pressure, though, I love my work. When I step out before an audience, I feel like I'm surrounded by my friends, living and dead.

By the time the curtain goes up, the energy is like white noise and individual thought patterns are popping into my head. Some people may have a preconceived idea that, before a show, I sit in my dressing room meditating in front of an altar or burning incense and chanting to spirit world to summon up my spirit guides. Sorry to disappoint but I'm more likely to be fussing about my hair! My work, connecting with spirit, is unaffected. I don't need to perform any magic rites or incantations. Why would I? That isn't what I'm about and never has been. I try to keep my show and my gift as genuine as possible. What happens to me happens naturally – or supernaturally, depending on which way you look at it. It's weird enough as it is: I've never felt the need to embellish it with any extra mysticism. In fact, quite the opposite: I try to analyse what I do scientifically – but I'll go into that a bit later.

For now, the best description I can give is that, when I start to receive messages, it's as if I take on the thought patterns and the memories of the person who is dead, as if these are dropped into my head. As you can imagine, it's not the easiest thing to describe, and I'm sure any psychiatrists reading this will be pulling on their white coats and knocking on my door pronto. It's not like the inner dialogue we all have inside our minds. That is conscious thought, which is the way we all talk to ourselves internally. No, this is subconscious, involuntary thoughts. If I said the words 'ice cream' to you, the chances are you would have an image of a lovely ice-cream cornet floating in your mind. You didn't think to yourself, Now what does an icecream cone look like? What colour is it? What does it taste like? Your mental image of an ice cream just popped into your head. That's how it happens with me. The thoughts are not mine, they belong to someone else but, because that someone else does not possess the ability to speak in the way we recognize, they use me as a mouthpiece instead. It's as if a trap door is opened in the crown of my head and all these random thoughts and memories are poured in and then they spill out of my mouth, like in a Monty Python cartoon.

The skill, and the thing that I have become much better at since I've been on the road doing my live theatre shows, is the ability to focus on specific messages and energies within the cloud of spirits and to shut out others. It's as if I can put a bouncer on that trap door who allows the messages to come in one or two at a time rather than all together. Imagine that kind of psychic energy flowing through you for three hours without regulation. I'd end up a gibbering wreck. Even as it is, the force of nature I feel flowing through me is explosive. After each show, having been plugged into the psychic mains for several hours, you could virtually scrape me off the ceiling. It takes me two hours to come down because of all that collective energy. I wish I could say it leaves me exhausted and that I sleep like a baby but, unfortunately, the opposite is true. I'm buzzing so much it often leaves me nursing a bout of insomnia, my mind racing and unable to shut down. Sometimes I wonder what the long-term effects will be. It could give me longevity – that's what I'm hoping: I certainly feel younger since I've been experiencing this energy in such large amounts. I feel energized after each show. I feel as if I've been shocked with a defibrillator every night. Then again, it could kill me – who knows? Speak to me when I'm a hundred and I might have a better idea! Can you imagine? I'll be in a home somewhere and the staff will be saying: 'See that woman over there? She reckons she used to be friends with the Princess of Wales and she speaks to dead people. She's nutty.'

The ability to regulate the thoughts and feelings popping into my head isn't a wholly conscious action. I can't choose the messages I receive. I can't reach in and pluck out specific thoughts or invite in specific spirits. It's not like choosing raffle tickets from some great psychic tombola. But when specific messages drop into my head I can concentrate on them and hold the others at bay. I can help them be heard. It's almost a reflex action, like moving an arm or a leg. You don't consciously have an inner dialogue with the muscles of your arm to instruct them what to do, it just seems to happen, allowing you to get on with other things, like chatting on the phone or doing your shopping. It's the same with me. To a degree, I can orchestrate the messages from spirit and stop the spirit energy overwhelming me while, back on earth plane, I speak to the audience, give a performance and act like a normal human being . . . well, normal-ish!

When I'm on stage, as those thoughts and memories drop into my head, I tend to take on the characteristics of the spirit that is supplying them. So I might suddenly develop a limp, or a squint. An opera singer came through to me recently and, without even realizing, I found myself straight-backed with a theatrically puffed-out chest. It's a little like being possessed, but there's no malice in it. My head doesn't spin around. As far as I can tell, it's just that, with the amount of practice I've had, my gift is developed to the point where the messages and personalities that come through to me now are so clear it's not just my mind that is affected, my body is too. Think, for example, of an athlete who trains for years to be a shot-putter. The most important muscles he or she develops are the ones around the arm and shoulder that will be doing the throwing, but the rest of his or her body develops too. The part of my brain that communicates with spirit has become increasingly developed over the years because I use it so much, but I reckon other pathways have opened up through my body as well which allow these psychic neurons to zip in and affect my arms, my legs or my face.

After the chaotic psychic orchestra of a show, those

pathways take a little while to close. After each show I do book signings and what we call meet-and-greets in the foyer. It gives me a chance to say hello to my lovely fans. The funny thing is that, because I'm so 'switched on', whenever I shake a hand or give a hug – any physical contact – I get a jolt of energy like a small electric shock from the person I touch and *bam!*, suddenly I know something about them, and I blurt it out.

'I'm sorry to hear about your job,' I'll say. Or: 'You wanted a message from your mum, didn't you, love? Don't worry, she's with you and she's proud of you.' They're often as surprised as I am. If I had a pound for everyone who has stood open-mouthed and asked me, 'How on earth do you know that?', I'd be a rich woman by now.

The truth is, I'm not entirely sure myself, but my theory is that spirits are always with us and around us, and they know everything about us; they know what we are getting up to, where we've been and what we've done. They exist in a very different place to the world we inhabit. They aren't constrained like we are to the physical world; they aren't bound to the past, the present or the future. They're not held down by space or time and they're attuned to the ones they love. So when I get a seemingly random message about a new pair of shoes someone might have just bought and I blurt it out to the new owner of those shoes, it comes from spirit, and it is that specific spirit's way of saying, 'I'm here, this is the proof.'

I'm not a mind reader and, thankfully, I can control this inbuilt psychic tuner, to an extent. So when I'm queuing up to buy my groceries in Tesco, I'm not looking around at all the other shoppers and being shown what they got up to the night before. Heaven forbid! If I started doing that I'd be the most unpopular woman in the country. It's not my business and, frankly, I don't want to know. I've also made a very conscious effort not to pick up spirit at home and not to invite in spirits connected to me or to my family. I feel it would make my personal life too complicated. It would drive my husband, John, and daughters, Fern and Rebecca, mad if I kept my psychic radar switched on all the time. After all, at the end of the day, we all need to have boundaries and I'm not sure I'd want passed relatives constantly contacting me, no matter how much they are missed. So, most of the time, the messages I pick up are for people in the audience. I think my friends and family in spirit probably recognize this and respect my wishes. Mainly, they stay away. They know they will see me again one day, and in the meantime they leave me to do my work. Well, they do most of the time anyway, but the thing with spirits is that they come to us when we need them.

A Spirit, My Saviour

Before I tell you about the time I was saved by a very unexpected visitor, we need to clear up something. We need to address the elephant in the room, as the saying goes. That elephant was me. Until the beginning of 2009, I was morbidly obese. I was 'Psychic Sally: Medium at Large'. I've heard them all, believe me. I was 'larger-than-life Sally Morgan'. Every label I was given seemed to relate in some way to my size. I was a headline writer's dream thanks to my profession – medium – because, in reality, I was an extra-large.

Here is not the place to go into detail about how and why I got to the size I did but, suffice to say, at my heaviest, I was 23 stone. I was suffering increasingly bad health, each year I was developing bouts of pneumonia and I was having mobility problems, which were exacerbated by the hours I spent standing on stage. I had constant aches in my hips and knees and, some days, the effort of simply walking from my dressing room to the stage sent waves of agony through me.

One night in early 2009, I was about to go on stage in a theatre in the north of England. Everything about the day had run like clockwork. John and I had driven up to the venue in the car from our home on the outskirts of London. Sitting in my dressing room, I applied my make-up and checked my hair, just as I'd done countless times before.

For anyone who has seen the TV series *Psychic Sally: On*

the Road, you'll know I have a production team who arrive at each venue and set up the equipment. I don't have a stage set like at a rock concert but we do have the camera and sound equipment, the video screen and a stage backdrop, as well as baskets for letters and photos and an audience video-message facility to set up. While I'm getting ready, the crew busy themselves with the technical stuff. About an hour before the show begins I have my quiet time, where I'll sort out the final details, and then, ten minutes before the show starts, Julie will knock on my dressing-room door and let me know it's almost curtain-up time.

This particular night, she called out like every other.

'OK, love, I'm ready,' I answered.

She's my little pre-show angel is Julie. She makes sure I get to the stage in plenty of time and in one piece, and gives me the once-over before I step in front of the audience to ensure I look presentable. It's thanks to Julie that I don't step out on stage with stray labels hanging out of my clothes or my skirt tucked into my knickers. She's always there with her little pink torch, ready to guide me through the corridors of whichever theatre we're in to the side of the stage.

That night, as we walked off, I started to feel a pain, as usual. Not a terrible, agonizing pain but a niggling ache in my hips. It had nothing to do with pre-stage nerves, it was to do with my size. At the time my weight was hovering around 20 stone which, coupled with my diminutive height, meant I was dangerously overweight. In fact, I was morbidly obese. To put it in black and white, I was in danger of killing myself with food. That ache was my hip telling me I wasn't getting any thinner.

Of course, I'd always been aware of my size. I wore size 26 to 28 clothes – I couldn't really deny it. But it had never particularly bothered me. It was part of who I was, part of what I was, and I was happy with myself. I was confident and successful. My size didn't make me miserable. I'd been big for so long I accepted it as normal. I didn't agonize over diets and calorie intake. I didn't look in the mirror and weep. The trouble was, even though I was happy being who I was, my body wasn't happy. It was decidedly unhappy. And it was increasingly telling me how unhappy it was.

At this point, I'd been touring for a year, spending up to three nights a week standing on stage and more hours than I care to remember cooped up in cars. My joints were really starting to suffer. And those walks through the warrens of backstage theatre corridors, up and down narrow staircases, were becoming harder and harder.

Most nights, I'd reach the stage wings out of breath. I'd have to stand there and have a short rest before bounding on stage to meet my public. Only, increasingly, I wasn't bounding, it was more of a hobble, and every now and then, when I should have been meeting the audience with a wide, friendly grin to make them feel at ease, the first thing they saw was a grimace as the pain in my hips flared up and reminded me that they could only take so much punishment. God knows what the people in the front row must have thought when the stage lights went up: Who's this nut-nut wincing at us?

Julie got used to it over time. Gradually, through the months of the tour, I'd started to lean a little more heavily on her for support. My breath had become laboured;

often I'd give a grunt of pain. In theatres with several corridors to walk down and several sets of stairs to negotiate, the walk to the stage felt like a climb up Everest, not a stroll from the dressing room. These external, physical problems were just the tip of the iceberg, though. You see, there was a killer lurking in my family history – heart disease. And my expanding hips and waistline were inviting it in.

My birth father, Derek, had died of a stroke brought on by heart disease, aged sixty-seven. His two brothers, my uncles, had also died of heart disease. Uncle Bobby was just forty-two when he died, and Uncle Bill was in his early seventies and on the operating table about to have a stent fitted when he had a heart attack and passed away. I was just as predisposed to heart disease as they were, and they had not been as overweight as I now was. I was living on borrowed time. I knew that because, just over a year before, I had suffered a mild heart attack myself.

It's not something I've advertised but, in a wonderful twist of irony, I was in a London hospital having a checkup in a cardiology unit when, after wiring me up to a monitor, the doctor turned to me and said, 'Mrs Morgan, you are having a heart attack.' I couldn't have been in a better place and, thankfully, it was only a very mild one. However, it did mean I was then permanently on heart medication.

Anyway, on the night in question, the psychic buzz had been building, as it always did, getting louder and more excited as the start of the show drew nearer. As I stood with Julie in the darkness by the side of the stage, catching my breath and aching, listening to the video montage playing on the screen on stage, one thought, one voice popped into my head with such force and familiarity it took my breath away. And it kept reverberating around in my mind: 'You can't go on like this, Sally. You can't go on like this, Sally.'

I still remember it so clearly, as if it were yesterday. It was a male voice, stern and authoritative, but also full of love and concern. And I knew straight away who it was – my grandfather, George. He was Mum's dad, and a lovely man. We'd shared a special bond when he was alive. He ran newspaper stands and owned a big working men's cafe in Hounslow, Middlesex. I used to work for him every Saturday and throughout the school summer holidays through most of my teens. He lived for his horse racing and loved a punt on the gee-gees. He always had the racing papers and studied form like it was a science.

But he had died many years before and, on that night, he had returned, and he was telling me that if I didn't sort myself out, all bets would be off. He was warning me that I'd reached the limit of what my body could cope with, and that if I didn't do something drastic, and quickly, I'd be joining him in spirit. It was like a light coming on in my head. It was my epiphany, and the moment I realized that I was dying. I was eating myself to death. I also realized that larger-than-life Psychic Sally's days were numbered – literally, if I didn't do something about my weight.

I must have gone pale, because Julie was looking at me with a frown on her face. She knew there was something wrong.

'You all right, Sal?' she asked.

'I can't go on,' I told her.

She panicked. 'What's wrong? Are you OK? Are you

feeling ill? The montage is about to finish, the theatre's full, everyone's paid and they're in their seats. What are we going to tell them?' she said.

'I don't mean I can't go on stage,' I reassured her. 'I mean I can't go on like this,' I said, pointing at myself. 'I have to do something and I need to do it now.'

And with that I walked out on to the stage, leaving Julie standing there in the wings in the dark wondering what the hell I was going on about.

That night Grandpa George had made sure his message came in loud and clear and that he got his voice heard before all the other messages came in. He certainly rammed his point home. He was a funny man and full of warm humour but when he was alive, when he was telling you something, you listened. And he hadn't lost that ability in death. After that show, I got home in the early hours of the morning and looked up the number of a bariatric surgeon I had been in contact with a few years previously. The following day, I called him, booked an appointment and, within a year, had undergone life-saving gastric-bypass surgery. I'm a shadow of the woman I used to be, and thank God for that. I lost 11 stone in the nine months after the operation, I wore a dress and heels for the first time in thirty years thanks to my incredible weight loss and, more importantly, I reclaimed my life and got my health back.

Every one of us has people in spirit, and they look out for us constantly. Their souls are made of an energy that defies current scientific classification. That energy watches us, it waits and, at times of peril, it supports us. Grandpa George was there for me that night; his energy pushed through and he saved my life.

Just a Normal Girl

When I was a little girl growing up in Fulham, south-west London, I never considered my childhood anything other than normal and, in a lot of ways, it was normal. I had a close, loving family. I had lots of relatives and lots of friends. I had the type of freedom my generation took for granted. We were latch-key kids: we played outside, we found our fun and adventure in the streets of London, which seemed much safer and friendlier than they do now. There was a tight-knit community in Fulham in those days and everyone looked out for each other. You knew who your neighbours were, you knew what they were up to . . . sometimes, people knew too much. If us kids were misbehaving on the streets, one of the adults in the road would give us a telling-off or a clip round the ear. You can't do that now – you'd end up in court. I know I sound like a grumpy old biddy, but I'm not sure now whether things have got better or worse for children. When I look at my grandchildren, I almost feel sorry for them. On the one hand, they have so much more than people of my generation, what with their iPods and Wiis, but on the other hand, so much less – less freedom, less security. They will never be allowed the amount of freedom we had as children and I wonder how that will affect them as they grow older. At the age of five, we were allowed to ride around the pavements on our bikes and go and buy groceries for our parents down the local shops. You wouldn't dream of allowing children so young to do that now.

So that was normal Sally: a little girl growing up like any other little girl. But then of course there was abnormal Sally: the one who saw things no one else could see; the one who had an invisible friend in the art cupboard in the classroom at school that no one could hear; the one who knew things about people there was no way she could or should know; the one who heard voices no one else could hear.

As far as I was concerned, all this spookiness was no big deal. People often ask me when I first realized I was different from everyone else; what was my big epiphany? Well, I didn't really have one. My gift, if you like to call it that, had always been with me. I had always been aware of it. It's not as if, one day, I suddenly started seeing things. I just grew to realize I was different over time, not because I had a sudden awareness but because I gradually became aware that other people didn't have the same ability that I did and that when I told them what I felt and saw and heard, it often made them uncomfortable.

Even when I started to realize I had a special ability, it didn't affect the way I was as a child. I didn't suddenly start to wear dark clothes and lock myself in my room with the curtains pulled. And it didn't scare me. It surprised me on many occasions, and it still does, but it never frightened me. The dead are not here to scare us (evil is very rare in the afterlife), the dead are here because they love us, so even though I have been shown some awful things by spirits, they have not intended to upset me. The content of signs they give is intended to validate the identity of the spirit giving those signs.

I'd often run to Mum in our house in Waldemar Avenue and tell her excitedly, 'I've just seen a man upstairs. His face is all burnt,' or, 'That boy over there just touched my shoulder.' Or I'd sit down for breakfast and tell her about the dream I'd just had that something was going to happen.

'I had the strangest dream,' I'd say. 'I dreamt that a car knocked down the front wall at number 58.' And, sure enough, a few days later a car would skid in the road and bump into the brick wall at the front of number 58. Mum never discouraged my gift or told me to stop being silly.

Looking back now, I realize that my gift was often in tune with the physical condition of my body. If I was feeling ill, if my resistance was low, I'd have more intense experiences. And I was a sickly child. I had a shadow on my lung when I was little, and this left me predisposed to respiratory problems. I had whooping cough regularly when I was growing up, and before my gastric-bypass surgery I was prone to chest infections throughout winter. Maybe my conscious mind held the spirit side at bay but weakened if I got ill and let the subconscious take over. The same process happens in people who have inherent physical weaknesses or long-standing ailments such as arthritis: it usually becomes worse when they are under the weather. When I was younger, I had a squint, and that too always got worse if I was coming down with something. So, whenever I came down with a cold or a tummy bug, not only would I be squinting, I'd also be seeing dead people more intensely in my mind's eye. It's a wonder Mum didn't call in the child psychologist!

When I was teenager and my body began to change like every other teenage girl's, I started to experience even more intense messages. When I was fourteen, I heard a man's voice in my bedroom. Before that, the things I heard were in my mind. I suppose my psychic radar had not developed enough at that time to tune into the energy. But this time it wasn't a soft voice in my head; it was so pinpoint, crystal clear it sounded just like an actual voice, as plain as if my dad had been in the room talking to me. And, my God, did it make me jump. You'd think that, by then, I'd be used to strange things happening, but this was like taking a step up to another level. All my life, strange things had been going on in my head, but the things I heard were like muffled thoughts in the back of my mind. This was totally different. Even now I shiver when I remember it. Today, after years and years of developing my gift and living with it, I understand it better and I'm able to control it, up to a level. Back then, any new occurrence was a step into the unknown. I'll take that first audible voice to the grave with me.

A few years later, after I left home and was working as a dental nurse in a clinic, we had a spirit in the house who used the record player to communicate. And he wasn't impressed with my taste in music. Again, he had an energy strong enough to come through as clear as a living voice, and strong enough that other people would pick it up too. I remember very clearly the first time we heard him. Mum and I were listening to records on the old player we kept in my uncle Derek's bedroom. It was a grey autumn Saturday afternoon, and as I reached over to take a Cliff Richard 45 out of its sleeve, an angry voice echoed in the room.

'Shut that bloody racket up,' it said.

By this time I was at ease with the messages I picked up from spirit, but my mum was spooked. She couldn't understand where the voice came from. We were the only ones in the house and I was no ventriloquist.

Most of my friends were spooked by my house too. It was a big old house, and in that part of London there weren't many of them left. You see, in the late fifties and early sixties in London, everything was in a state of transition. The war had finished over a decade before, but it took many years to clear and rebuild the heavily bombed areas of London. As the old houses were cleared away, they were replaced with new flats, and the whole of London seemed to be changing, transforming itself out of the old world and into the new. The landscape I grew up in was a mish-mash of old Victorian and Edwardian townhouses, bombed-out derelict houses, building sites and new flats. Most of my friends lived in the new parts of Fulham where the council had cleared the bombed properties and built new council estates. They would come to my big old house and say, 'Sal, aren't you scared living here in this old house?' But I didn't know any different.

My house was haunted, no question about it. As well as the man in my room and the man who communicated through the record player, I also felt the spirits of several women living with us. Years later, I researched the history of 13 Waldemar Avenue and learned that, decades before we moved in, it was inhabited by a man, his wife and his four daughters. They all grew up there, and the daughters left and married but all ended up divorced and returned back to the family home. I like to think they were independent, strong women because, back in those days, you never got divorced; if your old man was knocking you around, you just got on with it. It took a very strong-willed woman to walk away from a marriage, no matter how miserable it was. I also like to think that the house had its own special magnetism which drew them back, and that, after they died, they had such a strong psychic link to the property they never really left. Our family was sharing the house with them, and the odd thing was that our family history mirrored theirs in a lot of ways. My mum grew up there, left, got married and divorced and moved back, and so did I, just like the daughters.

The family was not malevolent in any way. They loved the house and they loved us. I know this for a fact because, years later, when my mum sold the house and moved out, after just three weeks the place burnt down. They never found out what caused the fire. All they knew was that the fire had started in my old bedroom.

My First Experience of Grief

Like most children, my first experience of human death was the loss of a grandparent: my grandma, Nanny Gladys. To this day it saddens me that I was so young when she passed. I was just four, and I have no firm memories of her. However, I do know she was an amazing woman. In Fulham she was a legend, one of those larger-than-life personalities you only seem to find in soap operas nowadays. She worked hard did Nanny Gladys, and in those days it was unusual for a woman to be out working; unless you were a teacher or a nurse, there just weren't the opportunities us girls have nowadays. Most women would stay at home raising the children, doing the housework and preparing their houses for when their husbands got home. It seems so quaint now, doesn't it? I could never imagine myself chained to the cooker or the iron . . . especially the iron!

Nanny Gladys was a multitasker. She managed to keep the house spick and span, look after her children and grandchildren and be a businesswoman too. She was a trail-blazer, I suppose, a feminist long before anyone knew what a feminist was. She was one of the first women I know who proved that you can have it all – a career and a family – and she didn't have any help, she didn't have a cleaner or an au pair. As well as being the family matriarch and the glue that held us all together, she went out and did a man's job. She was a newspaper seller on the pitches that she and Grandpa George ran in that part of London. They owned four stands around Fulham and Chelsea, and in those days you could earn a half-decent living selling papers to City workers, not like today when they are given away free. Nanny Gladys would be out in all weathers at the pitch she ran in the entrance to Putney Bridge station, with her piles of *Evening Standards*.

I never really knew her because I was so young when she died. I have snatches of memories, though. I remember how she used to sing all the time, her voice filling the house. I remember her encouragement when I started to take my first steps and how she'd look after me in the day sometimes when Mum went to work. I have this image of her in my mind: tall and slim, hunkered down inside her padded coat, yelling the day's headlines to the commuters as they got on and off the trains.

My mum would always talk to me about her as I grew up. After the war, everyone valued their freedom more than ever, and Nanny Gladys embraced hers and worked hard to provide for her family. She was outgoing and sociable too, so she loved to pass the time of day with the people at the station, catching up on the community gossip. The world was a lot smaller then, and everyone knew everyone else. Nanny Gladys was one of the lynchpins of the community. If you wanted to know what Mrs Jones from the launderette had been up to, Nanny Gladys had the info. If you wanted to know who the strange man was who visited number 42 when the man of the house was at work, Nanny Gladys would be able to tell you.

But Nanny Gladys's gift for knowing what went on in

the community didn't come just from idle gossip. You see, she had a special ability, the same type of ability I seem to have inherited when I was born. Nanny Gladys was a medium. She knew things about people she shouldn't have known. Just by brushing someone's hand when they passed her the money for their evening paper she'd be able to tell deeply personal things about them. It was as if the spark of a secret had jumped from their hand to hers in that brief contact. How do I know it worked like that? Well, it's exactly the same thing that happens to me.

From what my mum told me, Nanny Gladys didn't hide the truths she knew either. If someone was up to no good, she'd let them know she knew about it. If they had a health problem, she'd wish them well. 'Hope those piles clear up, Norma,' she'd say, and then probably put her hand over her mouth in mock shock and try to hide the sparkle in her eye. She was a mischievous one was Gladys, and even though she upset plenty of people with her inexplicable knowledge, and scared just as many as well, she was well thought of in our neighbourhood. She was a regular in the local and would pop in every night after work for her one treat of the day: a glass of Guinness. She'd laugh and joke with the other locals as she perched on the bar stool that was always waiting for her and then she would come home and make sure everyone had a hot tea.

They called her the Witch of Fulham, but it wasn't meant in a nasty way, not at all. It was a term of endearment. She was one of life's characters was our Gladys, a ball of energy and personality: fiery, passionate and good-humoured in equal measure. It's no wonder she had the gift. She was full of life, you see. She had such amazing life force that it acted like a beacon, shining out of her heart and drawing the spirits around her like a gravitational force. I truly believe that this is the case with real mediums. It is not the gift that creates their personalities; it is their personality that heightens their psychic ability. Humour, compassion, love, passion, openness, laughter – all those positive qualities that draw people to us in the living realm also attract spirit. That's often the way it works: things that ring true in life also ring true in death. As you'll learn through this book, the differences between the living and the dead are not so great. The qualities that are intrinsic to us here on the earth plane are also important to those who have passed. They hold just as much currency after death as they do in life.

So Gladys was a spirit magnet. The living loved her and the dead did too.

Her funeral remains one of my earliest memories. It was the flowers that burnt it into my memory. A house full of flowers, so many of them that the sweet smell was overpowering, almost intoxicating. They filled the hallway and the front room and the pavement outside the house. Nanny died of septicaemia when she was just forty-one, and my family – Mum Beryl, father Pat and sister Gina – were distraught. But no one more so than Mum.

She was so young when Gladys died she just couldn't come to terms with it. She was wrapped in anguish. So as well as being my first experience of death, Nanny's passing was also my first experience of grief. It was not my own grief; I was still too young to fully understand the feelings of loss I was experiencing. As far as I was concerned, Nanny was now in Heaven, which by all accounts sounded like a lovely place to be. When you're four years old, you can't fully grasp the concept of never actually seeing someone again. Kindly family members would say, 'It's okay, love, you'll see her again one day; you'll be together in Heaven.' And to the mind of a four-year-old with little grasp of the reality of lifespan and time, that meant I'd see her maybe in the next few weeks.

Even though I was too young to understand the feelings I was experiencing, I still remember seeing Mum weighed down by a dragging pain, full of yearning for the person she would never see again and full of regrets for the things she'd never had the chance to say to her own mother. I couldn't rationalize what I felt when I saw Mum upset but I distinctly remember it making me feel uncomfortable and insecure. It's only later in life that we start to realize just how painful grief is.

Of course, today grief is an emotion I deal with on a daily basis. Every time I stand on stage and begin the process of channelling messages between the living and the dead, I encounter grief and, as far as I'm concerned, it can be one of the most destructive emotions you can ever experience if you let it. For those grieving without hope, it can be all-consuming: that empty, hopeless feeling can manifest and fester, especially when a loved one has been snatched away too early. Over the time I've been working as a professional medium, I've encountered more extreme cases of grief-ruined lives than I care to remember. I've seen so many poor, wretched people held back from life and eaten up by their heartache.

Normally, grief is part of the natural healing process after loss but, in extreme cases, the hurt never heals. It just stays, lodged in the heart, growing like a cancer. That's why what I do for a living is so fundamentally important for people who find themselves trapped in a prison of grief. I can offer hope and reassurance that their loved ones are not lost at all; they have merely moved on in their journey to the next phase and they have taken their love with them.

As a four-year-old, I didn't understand any of this. All I knew was that Nanny Gladys was no longer with us and that made Mum very sad. I didn't know it at the time, but it was this sadness that would lead to my introduction to the world of mediumship.

A Spiritual Awakening

I'd never heard the term 'medium' before Nanny died. But in the years that followed, Mum, in her anguish, couldn't come to terms with her loss and began to look for answers. She was suffering raw grief, and anyone who has lost a loved one in tragic circumstances will understand this. She had great difficulty accepting what had happened and was weighed down with unanswered questions. For years, as I was growing up, she hunted for an explanation. Why did her mother die so young? Why did she leave her? Was she at peace? Did she suffer? Was she in a good place? The same questions apply to all deaths, and if these questions remain unresolved it's hard for the living to move on. This is why so many people come to me and to my shows. Each night a large percentage of the audience sits there hopefully, waiting for answers to questions like these. And back in the early fifties, you didn't have touring psychics, so the only place my mum could go to try to have her grief-laden questions answered was the Spiritualist Church. Spiritualism is a religion, a comparatively new one at that.

People have been fascinated by the idea of an afterlife and have been seeking evidence of it for thousands of years. In fact, the quest for an explanation of what happens to us after we die is probably as old as the human race. It's natural to want to know what death holds for us. You can almost imagine cavemen sitting in their caves millions of years ago gnawing on their dinosaur-bone dinners and grunting to each other about their afterlife theories!

Spiritualism was a movement that formed in response to society's inquisitiveness about the nature of life and death. To understand why it developed when it did, you have to know a little bit about the world in the early nineteenth century, when spiritualism first gained a popular following.

It was the age of the Industrial Revolution, a point in history when what we know as the modern age was first starting to develop. Great Britain, northern Europe and the USA were being transformed by new inventions and by science. People were fascinated with the world around them. Long-distance travel had become possible, thanks to developments in steam-powered technology, and ideas outside Christianity were just beginning to become known. Travellers came back with stories of different religions from all corners of the world.

Spiritualism developed in New York in the 1840s and quickly attracted a following throughout Victorian Britain, where mediums and their amazing powers were displayed to the public and hailed as one of the wonders of the age. At the time, although mainstream Christian churches were still attracting plenty of followers, there was a demand for answers, and this new age of endeavour and openness meant there was room for new philosophies to grow and develop. Spiritualism set out to use science as a way to prove that there was life after death.

Spiritualists often say that 31 March 1848 marks the true birth of their movement. On that day, two young sisters, Kate and Margaret Fox, who lived in a suburb of

New York, reported that they had made contact with the spirit of a murdered salesman in their house. The ghost communicated by knocking on the walls, and witnesses were amazed when the girls were able to demonstrate this phenomenon. The two Fox sisters began making public appearances, in which they would talk to ghosts, and eventually developed a travelling psychic show that took them across America and Europe. Although Margaret once said the sisters had used trickery – a claim she later retracted – general interest in Spiritualism, psychics and mediumship continued to grow. Spiritualist organizations were formed in the US and the UK. In London, the Spiritualist Alliance published its own magazine, *The Light*. And it was to this movement that Mum was drawn in her quest to cope with her grief over her own mother's death.

For a family that had grown up with 'the Witch of Fulham' as its matriarch, it was not a huge leap of faith to become interested in Spiritualism. I'm sure in most other households of the time, if anyone had finished supper and proclaimed, 'I'm off to the Spiritualist Church for a séance,' they would have been scorned, but not in our house.

As I grew older and my own psychic ability began to develop, Mum decided one day to take me to a Spiritualist Circle (the name given for a meeting in a Spiritualist Church). I was fifteen, and didn't really have a clue what to expect, but Mum wanted to take me along because, as I went through puberty, my strange 'knowings', as she called them, were becoming increasingly intense: the voices, the visions – all the spooky stuff a normal, well-adjusted preteen shouldn't be experiencing. It didn't worry me: as I've said before, it was something that had been with me from

44

birth, so to me it wasn't surprising. Mum realized that the ability I had was powerful and thought that I was old enough to go to a meeting and be introduced to her Spiritualist friends, so she took me to a place called Kelvedon Hall in London, on a night when a man called Joseph Benjamin would be there.

I had no idea what to expect. Mum had been going to Spiritualist Circles for years to try to contact Nanny Gladys, but she had never taken me along before. I remember feeling very grown up that evening. I had come home from school, had my tea and waited for Mum to give the order to go. Walking up to the blue doors of the community building, I had butterflies in my tummy. Once inside, though, they were soon replaced by disappointment. Maybe I had been expecting a hall full of young, exotic people, all drawn together by their search to answer some of life's most fundamental questions. All I found were a few oldies sitting on plastic chairs sipping watery tea from a stainless-steel urn and making polite conversation about the weather. They were probably only in their forties and fifties, which today doesn't seem that old but, from my teenage point of view, they were ancient.

Back then, middle-aged people didn't dress in the same clothes as teenagers as they do today. I wear tops that my daughter Fern would wear, but if you were forty and dressed like a youngster in those days, people would have thought there was something very strange about you. Consequently, as far as I was concerned, I was in a room of fogies. They were all dressed like Ena Sharples from *Coronation Street*, in coats and little hats.

I looked up to Mum with questioning eyes, but she just

looked down and smiled. It was then that I realized that everyone in the room was looking at me. What Mum hadn't told me was that, on that night, I was going to be the guest of honour. They had heard all about me thanks to Mum, and they were going to investigate my ability – in a nice way, of course, not like a lab rat being experimented on. But still, as a teenager, I wasn't over-excited at the prospect of spending an evening with a bunch of weird old people.

Joseph Benjamin, the man we had come to meet, was a well-known medium based in the area, and he held regular circles like this one. He walked across the hall to greet me and my mum. He seemed a kindly man, balding, with glasses and a dark, sober suit. He ushered me to a chair in the circle and, as he did, Mum turned around and left. So not only was I in a room with a bunch of strangers, I was now on my own. The evening was not turning out the way I'd hoped!

As I sat down, I remember catching sight of a man in the corner. He was half in and half out of the shadows, almost fully formed but not quite. He wore dark clothing and stood still, watching. I felt no fear, and he didn't look threatening at all. He was just quietly watching the evening unfold. I knew straight away he was in spirit. As I looked over at him, he looked at me and a small smile of recognition flickered across his lips. I didn't say anything to anyone in the room. Whenever I saw spirit, which was pretty much all the time, I accepted it. To me, it was unremarkable and, over the years, experience had taught me that often it was best just to keep quiet.

But, although I said nothing about the stranger in the corner, my eyes must have given something away – maybe I looked too long at the spot where the man stood – because when my gaze turned back to Mr Benjamin, he gave me a knowing smile and looked over to where I'd been looking. He saw the figure too.

And the night didn't become any more normal.

'We're going to open ourselves up to spirit, Sally. Is that OK with you?' asked Mr Benjamin. I nodded in agreement.

For the next hour, I was asked to look at each member of the circle and describe what I saw. Around each person, I could feel and see spirits. I could see their loved ones: husbands, wives, mothers, fathers and grandparents. As I looked from person to person, Mr Benjamin asked me to describe what I saw.

'I can see a man standing behind her,' I reported. 'He's wearing a jumper and part of the third finger on his right hand is missing. He walks with a slight limp and I can hear him speaking, although it's a bit unclear.'

'What is he saying?' asked Mr Benjamin.

'I think he's saying, "I love you, Marge. I'm with Uncle Tommy and I watch you when you cry at night."'

As I went round the room, explaining what I was see-ing and hearing, some of the people gasped, others cried. And they were encouraged to do the same to me: to look at me and to 'read' me.

Watching some of the other people in the room, I began to realize something. I began to see that, although they were trying hard to see things, they couldn't. Even though some of them were claiming to be mediums, they clearly weren't; they were clutching at straws, making wild guesses.

'I can see a man in a grey coat behind Joan. He has a beard and is carrying a rope,' one man said. I knew he was wrong because I could see a woman behind Joan.

At one point I was asked if I could see a man's aura. I've never seen an aura in my life; I don't believe there is such a thing. One of the men in the room said he could see mine. He described it as an orange glow, and I started giggling. His description made me sound like one of the kids on the Ready Brek packet.

After an hour, Mum came back to collect me, but before she did something odd happened. Mr Benjamin had obviously been impressed with me. He wasn't the type for overt scenes of enthusiasm; he had a sombre, serious air about him. But as the evening went on, each time I described what I was seeing and hearing, I would look to him for encouragement and he would give a little smile and a nod. I could see in his eyes that he was excited about something. He had 'the gift' and his was highly developed. He was recognizing a raw talent in me like that which he possessed when he was a boy, before he learned how to use it constructively. When the session came to an end, Mr Benjamin walked over to the chair I was sitting on, his eyes fixed on mine, and squatted down in front of me.

'You are me,' he said softly. 'You will carry on my work.'

I didn't have a clue what he was talking about at the time. I wasn't going to work in a stuffy hall with a load of oldies. I was going to be a midwife or a nurse. I didn't know about destiny or fate – the future I had mapped out in my head was in hospitals and clinics. It lay with the living, as far as I was concerned, not with the dead.

He could see the doubt in my eyes, and he reiterated: 'You will do what I do; you will be a medium.'

Although I didn't realize it then, Joseph Benjamin had a premonition that night and saw what I was to become.

It was a prophetic moment. It was that night that I started to understand who I was and what I could do. It was as if all the planets had lined up to determine my fate. Nanny Gladys's death had set it in motion all those years before, sending Mum on her quest for answers. Her search led her to that dusty hall and to Mr Benjamin, who recognized my ability, which I had probably inherited from Nanny. It was as if she was orchestrating events from beyond the grave.

I didn't grasp then that a form of psychic synchronicity was working that evening. I was a teenager more interested in John Lennon and the Beatles and getting home in time for *Top of the Pops*. What did I care about the hidden forces that guided the living and the dead?

All I knew at the time was that I never wanted to go back, and I never did. Joseph Benjamin believed in me, he could see my gift for what it was, he understood I was a medium like he was. Most people at the time, my family and friends, didn't share his belief. They wouldn't have said I was psychic. They would have said I was a romantic and a daydreamer, that I was prone to episodes of over-dramatization.

According to my school reports at the time: 'Sally has an amazing imagination. If she applies herself as much to her schoolwork as she does to her flights of fancy, she will do well.' This kind of thing has always been the medium's lot in life. People who do not believe in what we do will always criticize us. To them, at best, we are delusional and misguided; we have an overactive imagination. At worst, we are branded charlatans and con artists. I can understand why they draw these conclusions. Not everyone can understand what happens when spirits communicate with the living. It's an amazing, fantastical process and, probably, it will never be fully understood. Even I don't wholly grasp what happens when I'm on stage and the messages start to pop into my head, and I do it every night. I understand much more now about the process than I did when I was younger, but it still mystifies and amazes me. I can understand the doubters and the critics.

The one thing I really can't accept and which really upsets me are the sceptics who say that I and other mediums exploit people's grief. That accusation really angers me. I don't know why I was chosen to do what I do, but I do believe I was chosen to do it in the same way that someone who has a way with writing will become an author or a journalist. I also know that, night after night, people walk out of my shows with renewed hope in their hearts. When the messages are coming in thick and fast and I'm telling people things about themselves and their passed loved ones that there is no possible way I could know, they realize there is a greater power at work, and that gives them the validation and belief that there is a life after death and that their loved ones are happy and around them.

People come to my shows for all sorts of reasons. Many come just because they have seen me on the telly. But the bereaved come for comfort, for forgiveness, for confirmation. For example, at one show I picked up the spirit of an elderly man. He stood quietly on the stage by the side of me, and he was whispering a name.

'Leah, Leah,' he kept repeating. As I listened, the name Jack dropped into my head and I felt a burning sensation pass down the left side of my body. In my mind I could also see hair being snipped. I told the audience what I felt and what I was hearing. I always explain literally what is in my head, no matter how random it all seems; I don't try to interpret or edit the information I'm receiving because, often, even the most obscure things will mean something to someone.

A girl in front of me raised her hand and stood up. She was shy and petite, and I could see she was nervous.

'Don't be scared, love,' I soothed. Sometimes *I* get a bit nervous before I go on stage, and I've been doing it for years, so I have every sympathy for the people who stand up at my shows and get readings in front of an audience. Often the messages passed on to them are deeply personal. That night, for instance, there were over a thousand people in the theatre.

'What have I said that means something to you?' I asked the girl.

She explained that Jack was a man who used to live in the nursing home she worked at.

'Why am I getting cut hair?' I asked. 'He's showing me scissors.'

'I used to cut his hair for him,' she replied.

'I'm feeling hot, all down my left side,' I explained.

The girl, by now in tears, told me that Jack had fallen out of his chair and died. His body was discovered resting against a radiator. The girl, who had not been working that shift, had since felt an immense sense of guilt, because she had told him she would visit him but never got the chance to see him before he died. They were extremely close and she had always worried that he suffered and was in pain.

Jack came through that night because he could feel her hurt and he wanted her to know that everything was OK and that he was thankful for her care and her friendship.

This is just a small example picked from hundreds and probably thousands of messages I've been able to pass on over the years between the living and the dead that gave comfort and closure. They may not be around in a physical form that we understand, but the dead still care for us deeply and always will.

Religion and Rebirth

People often ask me whether I am religious. For the record, yes I am. But not in the conventional sense. I love churches, but I don't go to church; then again, I believe in many of the same things most religious people believe in. I was bought up in a Church of England household. We were not regular churchgoers, we didn't practise our faith at home, but we did go to church on family occasions such as weddings and christenings. I believe wholeheartedly in an afterlife — how could I not? The afterlife is what I do for a living. I see and speak to dead people, they are around me all the time, I have a unique window on their world and so I am 100 per cent sure that death is not the end. It's just the beginning of a bigger journey.

I also believe that we each have a soul or a spirit . . . different people call it different things. Call it whatever you want, but I know there is a part of us all that leaves our flesh-and-blood body when we die and lives on. And I believe in a higher being, a higher energy: a God. Again, different religions call this different things. It is an energy that is in charge of the soul and the realm of spirit. I believe there is a plan for us all, that everything happens for a reason, no matter how obscure or upsetting or illogical it may seem. I believe that we all have a destiny with death and that, no matter what happens in between, the day you die is set in stone. It is as if we are all born with a sell-by date stamped on our souls. We have an allotted time here on earth and, once that time is up, there is nothing any of us can do to stay here. We're called to toddle off on the next part of the journey. I also believe that spirit resides in a place of peace and love and that we are reunited with our loved ones there after we die. Christians would call this Heaven; other faiths have different names for it: Nirvana, Tian, Jannah. In all faiths it has the same basic principles; it is a realm of paradise reached after we die.

So that is my faith system, my set of beliefs, and to some religious people who may be offended by what I do, they will sound very familiar. I think one of the main differences, however, is that, although I say they are my beliefs, I have a deeper acceptance than that. The word 'belief' suggests that there is an element of doubt. But I *know* these things are true because I see and feel them each day, and I hope that the work I do proves to many people that we don't just die, we are reborn in another form.

In life, we all have profound moments where our eyes are opened, and mine came the day I witnessed the birth of a soul into the afterlife. Imagine: one day you are busy getting on with your life and, all of sudden, something happens that proves beyond doubt that alien life exists. Say you were having your lunch in the park and a spaceship landed in front of you and ET hobbled out. You'd see everything in a whole new light, wouldn't you? Well, the same thing happened to me in a hospital ward in 1979. I was shown a soul leaving a body, and although before that I *believed* in life after death, after that I *knew*.

I was a nurse at the time, working at the South London Hospital for Women. My shift that day took me to the oncology ward. It was the last place on earth the patients in it would experience: it was where women in the advanced stages of cancer were taken to die. Deathly quiet, and with a silent air of foreboding, it was a place of reverence, full of the dying moments of extremely ill women. As I walked down the ward at the start of my shift, I passed a bed with the curtains drawn around it. Behind the curtains I could hear the faint breaths of the patient and I knew that she was not long for this world. I could feel her life coming to an end.

Her name was Anne and she had been administered her final dose of medicine, the strong morphine-based mixture they gave terminal patients in those days to ease their last hours. Along with one of the other nurses on duty that day, I pulled back the curtains to check on Anne. She was extremely frail and appeared lifeless. Her skin was sallow and stretched across her drawn face like tracing paper, pale and transparent. She was sleeping peacefully, taking shallow breaths that made the white sheets covering her rise and fall in a fitful rhythm.

There were a few cards on the cabinet by her bed, an untouched glass of water and a bunch of brightly coloured spring blooms in a glass vase. She looked peaceful. I glanced around and saw a man sitting in the chair by the side of her bed. He was looking at her intently and his hands were resting on his lap. I knew I was the only one in that space who could see him. He was in spirit, you see. And I also knew he was her husband and that he was patiently waiting there for her, waiting to be reunited with the woman he loved.

As nurses, we were taught that the last sense to close

down as death grew near was hearing. I moved to the side of the bed, leant over and whispered quietly to her.

'It's OK to let go now, love,' I told her. 'Your husband is here for you. He's come to take you.' I gently stroked her cheek and, as I did, her eyes fluttered ever so slightly, and she was gone. What I witnessed next will always stay etched on my memory.

Above Anne, the air opened up. It started as a pinprick of light and grew slowly bigger, like a flower opening. I could *feel* the light; it filled the room with an amazing sense of peace and love. And as this light in the air opened I saw Anne's spirit leave her body. It was not in a recognizable human form – it was like a ball of bright white gas that drifted from her chest. As it lifted out of her, I felt a breath. The faintest hint of a breeze blew across me. It was warm, like a sigh. It was her essence, and it rose slowly and steadily towards the other light in the air. I stood fixed to the spot, in awe of what I was witnessing. And, as Anne's spirit rose from her dead body, the man sitting with her, her loyal husband, changed form. First, a glow surrounded him, like a halo. It became brighter and brighter and, as it did, the features I saw initially, his human form, became absorbed by the light and melted into it until it too became a ball of what appeared to be glowing gas. This rose to join with the spirit that had emerged from Anne, and together they became one and drifted slowly into the air and up to the glowing light. It took just seconds and, as slowly as the process started, that light shrank down and down, never losing its brightness until it became just a tiny pinprick of brilliance in the air. And then, as suddenly at it had appeared, it vanished. All that was left was me, my colleague, who had witnessed none of this, and the body of Anne, still and at peace.

I knew then that I had been privileged to witness something so fundamental and beautiful that I would never see it again. I had seen something so important: I had seen how life bridges death. To this day, I believe that there was a healthy dose of fate intervening that day. Why, of all people, was I there that day? I wasn't supposed to be on a shift and was covering for another nurse who had fallen ill. Surely it wasn't just luck that I, a medium, happened to be in that space at that specific time. I believe I was being shown how spirit worked. It was a sign. It was encouragement. It was something saying, 'There you go, Sal, that's what happens.' I might have believed in life after death long before that day, but on that day, in that hospital ward, I was given all the evidence I needed to have faith in my work, and whenever the sceptics question me now I think back to that day and those events and they reinforce my faith in what I do.

Of course, today, we are all a little more enlightened than in the past. The psychic business is booming, whereas, in years gone past, mediums like me were persecuted. A few hundred years ago I would have been labelled a witch and burnt at the stake or drowned in the duck pond on the village green near my house. I'm sure there are still a few people who would like to do that to me now.

I'm sure, too, there are religious people out there who would say that what I do is unholy, an abomination even. However, despite the critics, most people I meet are fascinated by it, even the religious ones. More often than not, they are polite and inquisitive. Sometimes I sense they are uncomfortable with it, but I've never been heckled.

If I worried about it too much, I wouldn't be able to do what I do. As far as I'm concerned, if you're making an omelette, you're going to have to break a few eggs. It sounds harsh, but us mediums, the genuine ones who have been imbued with an ability since birth, have to develop thick skins. When you deal with a subject as tricky as life after death, there will always be people who do not want to hear what you say. I wouldn't imagine I have many religious leaders in my fan base!

Several years ago, I was filming a documentary on religion in the USA, and the plan was for me to interview a series of religious leaders about their faith and the details of their beliefs. The plan was to speak to a Protestant, a Catholic, a Muslim cleric, a rabbi and a Baptist minister. However, the more we researched, the more we were knocked back.

'You must be kidding,' we were told. 'Even by agreeing to discuss the subject we could be seen by our congregation to be endorsing your views.'

Basically, because of what I do, I was seen as a heretic. No one except the rabbi would agree to go on camera with me. That's the thing with religion, especially when those who practise are very devout: it is inflexible. Most religions are closed systems; they aren't open to new ideas, even if they are based on evidence and experience.

I don't actually think we talk about religion enough, probably because at its heart is a taboo subject: death. It has always surprised me that many religions nowadays fail to address fully their theories of life after death. I suspect this is because there is a bit of a backlash at present against the idea of life after death. You can pick up plenty of books that discount religion and use science as a weapon against the idea that there is life after death. I sometimes feel it is as though religions are so under the cosh they are embarrassed to set out their arguments when it comes to the supernatural, even though the basic building block of most religions is the idea that there is another existence beyond this one. It's as if the whole issue is swept under the carpet.

I, on the other hand, regularly go on stage in front of a thousand people and talk very openly about life after death. I embrace it and, hopefully, I make it acceptable and in a small way counter some of the arguments against it. You could say I am the acceptable face of life after death.

I'm well aware that people with a vested interest in religion are wary of me. It's understandable because, ultimately, the work I do negates much of the mysticism that many religions wrap themselves in and it also questions some of the beliefs and practices that different religions have. For example, the Catholic Church believes that suicide is a sin that is punished after death. I can see why: the Catholic Church believes in the sanctity of life. But I know that suicides are not punished. Night after night, I have messages from spirits who have been so sad and wretched in their lives that they have ended them. They often regret what they have done and they often speak of the guilt of leaving loved ones, but they are always in a good place and they always come with a feeling of peace and deep love. They come through because they want to explain their actions and make peace; they want to tie up the loose ends they have left in our world.

Whenever I have the opportunity to read for people with relatives who have taken their own lives, I am always humbled to be able to put minds at rest. I have experienced countless examples over the years. Several years ago, when I did personal readings at my home, I was visited by a lady – let's call her Debbie – who had lost her husband. I didn't know this when she first arrived of course. Dressed in a smart suit, with her blonde hair tied back in a ponytail, she sat down with me and, immediately, I could sense a deep sadness. I could feel her pain and heartache even though, on the outside, she seemed businesslike, almost emotionless.

I looked at her and straight away felt a constriction in my throat that made me want hold my head to one side. Behind her I saw a man. He was tall, slightly overweight, and I could sense a longing in him, a yearning that may have been regret.

'I have a man here,' I told her as I began to describe what I was feeling and seeing. Then a name popped into my head. 'Who is Peter?' I asked.

'He was my husband,' she answered.

'Why is my neck hurting?' was my next question. I had a feeling of swaying, like a pendulum. As I told her this, her tough exterior began to fall away and tears pricked her eyes.

'He hanged himself, didn't he?'

She nodded through the tears.

A feeling of regret filled me.

'He is so sorry; he didn't want it to happen, but he was in such a dark place. He felt he had no choice. He didn't know what to do. He couldn't see a way out,' I explained.

As we talked, I felt a connection of love flood between them.

'He never meant for you to see him like that,' I told her. 'He says that is his biggest regret. What does that mean?'

Debbie told me that she had returned from work one day several months before and found her husband dead in the hallway: swinging from the car tow-rope he had hanged himself with.

'Why did you do it?' she sobbed to her husband. 'Why did you leave me?'

Peter's spirit told me that he had felt a failure, that his business had been in trouble. The people who worked for him had been about to lose their jobs and he had felt that the life he had carved out for himself and his wife was crumbling away. He felt he had failed everyone.

'He wants you to forgive him,' I told Debbie. 'He loves you so much and he is so sorry for all the hurt and pain you are going through. He says you need to be strong now and he wants you to be happy.'

Debbie wept. 'I'll always love you, darling,' she sobbed. 'Of course I forgive you.'

I saw Debbie several more times, and each time some of her doubts and some of the anger she felt at being left by her husband in such a way were alleviated. I felt Peter was at peace too. He certainly wasn't burning in hell. His only pain was his regret that he had inadvertently hurt his wife with the manner of his death.

Some people would say this was sacrilegious, that Peter's should be damned for what he did, and that I should too, for dabbling in what some would – wrongly – describe as the occult. But I had never met Debbie before; I knew nothing about her or her circumstances. She chose to come to me and Peter chose to come to her. They both had a need: her for answers and him for forgiveness. It was a pure and touching process, a human process. There is nothing wrong with the need for love and contact. There was nothing sinful about them or the hundreds of other people I've been lucky enough to help, living and dead.

It's natural for people to be scared of the unknown and of spirits and messages that come from beyond the grave, of course it is. But I'm lucky enough to be able to say to people, 'Actually, I know a little bit about this stuff, because I get to speak to spirits every day.' There are people who hate that because they want to keep death and what happens afterwards as mysterious as possible.

Imagine the implications if it were widely accepted that certain behaviours in life had no implications after death? That suicide was not punishable, adultery was not punishable and neither were 'sins' such as greed and lust. Who doesn't like a nice lie-in on a Sunday, followed by a fry-up and then maybe a trip to the shops for a new pair of shoes or a handbag, even if you don't really need them? Well, if you do that, you've committed sloth, gluttony and greed. And if you're proud of your new shoes you can add pride to the list too.

I'm not saying for a minute that I think we should all go out and live decadent, depraved lives, but our actions should be kept in check by our own codes of morality, not a trembling fear of hell and damnation. The seven deadly sins correspond to human frailties; we are all susceptible to them. The spirits I channel every day were once normal people like you and I; they did normal things and led normal lives. They were imperfect in life, just like we all are.

They weren't saints – in fact, some of them far from it: boozers, crooks, gamblers, thugs . . . I've had them all. But the one thing they all have in common in the afterlife is a sense of peace and contentment. They are in a good place, no matter what indiscretions they may have got up to in life. The higher being that looks over us all is very understanding. When you are dead, to a large degree, unless you have a really evil soul and have committed terrible crimes, the slate is wiped clean.

For me, faith doesn't have to be connected to a set of religious beliefs and a specific doctrine. My faith is the knowledge of an afterlife and the knowledge that, after I die, my soul will live on in a place of peace and love. That kind of faith is as important to us all as vitamins are. Every single human being, no matter what their religion or what their concept of life, has the capacity within them to have this kind of faith, and it nourishes us with hope. An atheist, someone who believes that, after we die, there is nothing and that our loved ones end when they take their last breath, is like someone who is anaemic. Their diet is lacking that vital nutrient and eventually it will make them spiritually ill: they may need a transfusion of faith.

Plugging into the Psychic Mainframe

I've never doubted that what I do is genuine. After all, how do you explain the fact that, night after night, I tell a roomful of strangers random things that are happening in my head and, miraculously, someone in the audience understands exactly what I'm talking about? It stands to reason: I'm not making the details up. The audience proves again and again that the messages are genuine.

I have only ever once doubted what I was doing and whether I should be pursuing a career as a medium. You wouldn't think it to look at me when I'm hosting a show, but there was a time when I was very uncomfortable with my ability. I was racked by doubt and not sure whether I could continue my work as a medium. You see, for years I had been working from home, seeing clients on a one-to-one basis. They would call up and John would book them in. I would never ask anything about them. I didn't know who would be turning up. They'd arrive, and John would greet them, make them a cup of tea and then they would come into my office, the comfy room at home where I did all my readings, and we would sit and chat and I would open myself up to spirit. I never knew what would happen and why they had booked. Some came out of curiosity, some came to test me. But mainly they came looking for answers, for reassurance. I never had to advertise, I never had to court or chase clients, they just came. My reputation spread by word of mouth. One client would come and then tell her friends, and they would be so curious they would book too, and then they would tell their friends. It took many years, but by the time I made my first television appearances my list of customers had grown to such an extent that, at one point, I worked out that, if I booked in everyone who had made an enquiry, the waiting list would have been eighteen years. Eighteen years! I'm not kidding.

Now, I'm always thankful that, at my age, I am still able to work, but having that amount of clients was crazy. However, I've always been a grafter and, in the end, it wasn't the workload that daunted me. The issue that started to niggle and trouble me was that, day after day, I was dealing with people at their lowest and most vulnerable. The vast majority of the stories I heard were tragic. There were bereaved mothers, sons and daughters who had lost their parents, and people caught in the pit of despair, tortured by tragedy and unable to see a way back. And I empathized with each and every one of them, as I do today. I felt their pain. To be good at what I do you need to have studied hard at the university of life. You need to have a finely tuned understanding of what people suffer in everyday life, to understand grief and loss.

Being brought up in a very working-class household where we often struggled gave me a lot of empathy for others. If I'd been born with a silver spoon in my mouth, I couldn't relate to people. I try to be consistent with my compassion. I need to feel the anguish and the elation of the people and spirits I connect with. I think that helps in making the messages I get as clear as they are. I think spirit realizes that I am understanding and respectful. If I became anaesthetized to the suffering, I would lose my edge. I hope I'm always able to cry with people and feel their pain. Nowadays, it's a skill. Thanks to TV and the internet, it is so easy to become numb to suffering. You can go online now and see footage of people being executed. Kids can see this kind of stuff. There seems to be an insatiable appetite for violence and suffering, and it is not healthy. We are in danger of forgetting what it is to be compassionate and human.

I never doubted my ability, but I did doubt my mental strength to carry on. I'm only human after all. And that doubt was always exacerbated by the critics, the people who wrote things on websites and in newspapers and magazines questioning what we mediums do, accusing us of preying on people's vulnerability. I'm not complaining. It comes with the territory and, in my heart, I know that I don't prey on anyone. People come to me through choice and I work with honesty and truthfulness. I never asked to have this so-called gift and, for a time, I doubted whether I should be doing this work at all. In the end, the naysayers did not make me give in. Just seeing the comfort and the hope my work gave the hundreds of people I saw over the years made me realize that what I do is valuable and worthwhile. What the critics did do, however, was give me the motivation to investigate my work, to find reasons and to try to look at mediumship scientifically – to look for an explanation.

It wasn't until I started to present my live shows that I began to realize that what I was channelling was an energy, like electricity, a psychic energy that passed through me. This energy is in us and around us. It's what I saw rise from the cancer patient all those years ago on the oncology ward. It's what I connect with each night before I go on stage. It's what sits in each and every one of us, at our core. It is what love is. It isn't tangible; it's ephemeral, like a mist, like a power, a static charge that can be in all places at all times. It can be an individual phenomenon like an orb, or it can be a mass, an amorphous cloud that sings and hums. It is the very stuff of life, made of the love that we all carry with us during our lives and take with us on our journey after death. It can transmit messages like radio waves. It can be magnetic, attracting other energies. It has different characteristics in different settings and I've watched in awe as I've learned what this energy does and what it means.

When I tune into this energy, I'm connecting to spirit, to the souls of the dead. Each message carried by the energy is a little miracle, a gift from someone departed to someone living. That's why I have to be true to the message; I have to deliver it as I see and hear it, even at the risk of making myself look a bit of a 'nana!

It has only been by doing the live shows that I've been able to feel how powerful this energy can actually be. It sounds odd, but the moment I started conducting readings standing up, rather than sitting down at home, I began to take on the characteristics of the spirits I was channelling.

I started out holding readings for rooms of fifty or a hundred people at leisure centres and village halls. In one of my first appearances I was concentrating on a spirit who was whispering names in my mind.

'James. Rita,' he said.

As I recounted what I was hearing to the audience and carried on tuning into him, I became aware of a ripple of laughter. I couldn't understand what was so funny until a woman in the audience called out: 'You're walking just like him.'

I didn't realize it myself, and there was certainly nothing deliberate on my part about it, but I had started to stroll, bow-legged, up and down the stage . . . and I started whistling.

'That's just what he used to whistle,' the woman called again.

Her name was Rita, and she had lost her grandfather, James, several years before. He had been a bus conductor and spent his days strolling up and down the aisle of the number 14 whistling to the passengers. And now, as his spirit was flowing through me, I was adopting his characteristics, and his granddaughter thought it was hilarious, and so did the rest of the audience. John, who was standing at the back of the hall, was looking at me as if I was mad. I shrugged. What could I do? I couldn't help it.

With bigger audiences came more 'hits', as I call them, those incidents and messages that literally take your breath away; the names and the information that are so accurate they surprise even me. Even now, after doing hundreds of shows, I still squeal with excitement whenever I get a reading that is spot on. Every night I'm blown away by what happens on stage. People don't always understand that and think it's an act, but I am genuinely amazed. When I open myself up to spirit, I'm not orchestrating what happens. I take a step into the unknown, I'm a puppet being guided by forces I don't fully understand, so when everything clicks, as it usually does, and the hits keep coming, thick and fast, I'm in awe. The moment I lose that sense of surprise and become blasé about my work is the moment I should give up, because I also feel that spirit responds to that excitement. It responds to my personality and my sense of wonderment.

Mediumship is not an exact science – sometimes the messages I get are garbled, hazy and unclear – so when I get something perfectly right, my heart skips. I take it as a compliment from spirit world. It's as if they are rewarding me, as if they see that what I am doing is having an effect and, if they see that I have picked out the right receiver and the link is strong, they reward me with more information. It's almost like what happens when you train a dog. If the dog sits when you ask it to, you give it a biscuit. You could say that the messages are my biscuits.

I definitely now know that my psychic sense is something that has developed with practice. Since I began touring and connecting with vast numbers of people, the readings have become increasingly strong and more accurate. I'd love to feel that the popularity I've been enjoying on earth plane is mirrored in spirit. Wouldn't that be a blast? To be spirit world's favourite medium!

I'm slowly warming to the responsibility of what I do and looking at it and investigating what happens and why, dissecting my work, more and more. It's no good me saying: 'I am a medium because I am accurate.' Accuracy is brilliant but it isn't good enough. I've always been fascinated by my work and been prepared to look at what I do in an honest, open way. Where my work is concerned, I want total transparency.

And the best way I can explain what happens after we die and why I can speak to dead people is that we all have a soul, and that soul is made of an energy that lives on in a parallel realm that is still connected to us. Long ago, most of humankind lost the ability to maintain this connection, but it is still there as part of our instinct, our natural intuitiveness. So, sometimes, even though you may not regard yourself as psychic, you may feel a presence around you, you may feel a loved one who has passed or just think of them out of the blue. These are just your natural psychic instincts firing somewhere in your subconscious. They are making a connection with someone in spirit who is with you.

Mediums have a more keenly developed sense of this intuitiveness. I'm not sure why – we're probably just born with it. From my experience, I suspect it may be hereditary; I probably inherited mine from my Nanny Gladys. But if it is there that ability can be developed. If you exercise it enough, it gets stronger. And, as it gets stronger, spirits recognize it and are drawn to it. The energy they are made of has a magnetic quality. It is drawn to places of love and spirituality and to places inhabited by other spirits.

Have you ever wondered why churches and places of worship have that special feel about them? Even if you're an atheist, you can't deny that certain places do have a *feel* about them. Why is that? They're only bricks and mortar after all.

The feeling comes from the imprint of all those people tapping into the spiritual energy I am talking about. It doesn't matter what the religion is – Christianity, Islam, Hinduism, Buddhism – the places of worship all feel the same. They all emit a feeling of reverence, they feel like sanctuaries. Wherever you get groups of people who go to examine and express their faith and their spirituality, there exists this residual energy. It isn't confined to places of worship either. You can sense the same feelings at places such as the Wailing Wall in Jerusalem and the site of the collapsed World Trade Center in New York. These are areas where people have congregated and contemplated the big question in life: what happens after death?

So what makes this energy? What are our souls made of? The answer, I think, is love. I don't think we'll ever be able to put a chemical equation to it. I don't think scientists will ever be able to say: 'Your soul consists of 75 per cent carbon, 20 per cent helium and 5 per cent nitrogen.' It doesn't work like that. This energy that we all carry transcends chemistry and science. It resides in our body until we die then moves on to the next part of its journey, like a caterpillar turning into a butterfly.

I believe there are three parts to our journey: our life on earth plane, spirit world and, finally, what I'll call Divinity. When we die, we go to spirit world, which is a heavenly place, but beyond this, eventually, when we have earned our place, we end up somewhere rapturous. Some people, if they have done amazing and great things in their life, will go directly to Divinity.

Wrapped up in spiritual energy is all the love we have in life and all the love we have been given. It also contains memories and parts of our character, which is why, when I tune into spirit, those who have passed can implant their own memories into me and, to some degree, possess me so I take on their characteristics. They do this to validate themselves to the receiver. It's like a radio wave: we turn on the television or radio and it picks up sights and sounds from thin air. When you think of it, it's amazing. If we could conjure up someone from the Victorian era and show them a working telly, they would think it was a miracle, as they would the telephone, with which we are able to talk to anyone in the world. In the same way, what I do seems miraculous because we just don't understand fully the mechanics of it.

What I do does, however, display certain characteristics and patterns that mirror processes in our world. I've noticed that psychic energy has a gravitational pull. Spirits are drawn to the energy of other spirits. On the road, I started to notice that, if I was giving a reading that was strong and accurate, I would start feeling messages from other spirits that related to people in the audience close to the original receiver. So, for instance, I'd be speaking to a woman called Carol and I'd pick up her grandmother in spirit; there would be powerful energy flowing between us. Then other spirits would be drawn to that energy radiating out from us, and one of those spirits would spot a loved one a few seats or rows away and send messages out to them through me.

Another way I like to describe it is that the spirits are like birds using thermals to fly. They circle on the energy and hop through the audience on the energy of each reading until they find the person they have come to give a message to, because they know everything. They know when a loved one will be at a show.

When spirits hone in on each other's energy like this, it is almost as if they are living people butting in on conversations. They don't do it deliberately, but spirit is as eager to speak to you as you are to receive a message from it. And while all this is going on, I am the mediator – the medium in the middle. I only have one mouth (John would say: 'Thank God for that') but sometimes I feel I could do with half a dozen just to get out all the messages that are popping into my head.

This hijacking of readings often happens with the photographs and the messages people leave for me to use on stage. At the start of each show, in the foyer, we leave out a basket for people to leave photos of loved ones in. I pick them out at random during the show and it seems to act as a trigger for a spirit who recognizes them to make a connection with me. Thoughts and images drop into my head and I tell the owner of the photograph what I'm picking up. There are also slips of paper in the foyer for the audience to write messages on and I read these out on stage and again pick up messages from them.

Spirit is clever. It knows which photos and messages I will choose and who I am going to. And often I will start talking to someone about the photograph I have picked and what I'm saying will mean nothing to them – which would be a disaster, if it wasn't for the fact that 99 per cent of the time someone behind will raise a hand because the messages I am giving are for them instead. The spirit has sabotaged the reading. It's unbelievable how many times it happens, and it always makes me chuckle, because it shows that spirits can be just as mischievous as the living and, just like us, sometimes they go a little bit too far!

The Funny Side of Death

The show was at a theatre in the north of England. I was giving a reading for a lady in the audience and, as her messages were coming through, there were other voices echoing in the background, other spirits on stage eager to connect with their loved ones. One of them was particularly forceful.

'Anita,' I said to the woman I was speaking to. 'Who is Anita?'

She shrugged. 'I don't know an Anita,' she answered.

'I have a man here, he's showing me a bed, and I have the name Anita. He's quite excited, he seems . . . how can I explain this nicely . . . a little bit frisky!'

The audience laughed.

Then I felt something brush my arm. I jumped back. I've felt spirits before and it always startles me. Sometimes it's a gentle brush on my cheek or a nudge on the arm, but it's always unexpected.

'Oh, he just touched me,' I said. 'He just touched my arm.'

The woman shook her head.

Then it happened. The faintest touch on the back of my leg.

'Oh my God,' I shrieked. 'He's trying to touch me up!'

As the audience laughed again and I hopped around on stage, I noticed a raised arm four seats to the left of the woman I was talking to.

'I'm Anita,' said a sheepish-looking middle-aged woman.

As she stood up, I felt a hand slide up my leg and touch my bum.

I shrieked again. 'Oh my God, he's just touched my bum.'

The woman was chuckling. 'That'll be my Charlie,' she said. 'He was always doing that. He doesn't mean anything by it; he could never keep his hands to himself.'

'He'd better not try any other funny stuff,' I mock-warned, covering myself up with my hands.

She explained that Charlie was her husband, who had died several years before and, by all accounts, he was sometimes a bit too touchy-feely with the ladies when he'd had a drink!

When people pass, I believe they take some of their character with them in the form of memories. All souls are pure and predominantly good but, occasionally, when they come through to the living and to mediums like me, they display parts of the character they had on earth plane to help confirm who they are. Otherwise, how would we recognize them?

I've had plenty of spirits who come through to me reeking of booze; others who are surrounded by cigarette smoke. They are not sitting there in spirit world with a whisky and ginger smoking a packet of Silk Cut, they just choose to show those facets of their life on earth to let those who they want to contact know that it's them. Otherwise, if they all came through the same way, it would be hard to distinguish between them. I could have ten Teds in spirit who died of a heart attack. Without extra detail, I'd spend all night trying to match up the right Ted with the right member of the audience. But if one Ted

75

comes through with a squint or a limp or a particularly deep voice, he is easier to identify.

It's almost like meeting people at Arrivals in an airport. Spirits come wandering through Customs, and the audience is waiting there to meet them. They need to be paired up but, if they all looked the same, you'd just end up with hundreds of people and spirits milling around clogging the place up. If I were to stand at the door and hand each spirit a piece of card with their details on – 'This is John, he likes a drink, he worked on the trains and he died of a stroke' – it would make them easier to identify.

When those character quirks are projected on to me, it's an added bonus for the audience because they see me, little Sally, limping around on stage talking in a gruff voice. Luckily, I don't mind being laughed at!

You need to be able to laugh at yourself in this job, believe me. My son-in-law Darren calls me the David Brent of the spirit world because I can be just like the Ricky Gervais character in *The Office*, blundering around, doing silly actions. Sometimes I'm drawn off on a complete tangent – I'm sure the audience is just waiting for those eccentric moments! And, besides, the laughter helps enormously. Another thing I have learned over the years is that spirit responds very well to laughter. They are drawn to good feelings.

That is one of the reasons I have never been able to understand why some mediums feel they have to dress up what they do with a dollop of hocus pocus and a load of ritual.

I loathe the vocabulary that some mediums use. Some will say 'God bless you' after each reading. I have no right to say that, I'm not a vicar. I just try to be as normal as possible, because I feel spirit reacts better when people are being honest and open. I mean, I do love a candle, and I especially love a scented candle, but I don't need to light a candle to do my work. It wouldn't affect what I do. I just like the smell.

With all that gobbledegook, it's no wonder mediums are often ridiculed. Sometimes, the way we're portrayed in the media is less than flattering. However, over the last decade or so, I've noticed that things are getting better. Hopefully, people approach us with a more open mind than maybe they used to in years gone by. Films such as *The Sixth Sense* actually do us justice. I watched it and was wowed. For those of you who haven't seen it, it's about a little boy who is psychic. He sees dead people. I won't give away the twist in the ending, but I saw it and thought: 'This is my life story.' And there's a scene in the movie *Ghost* where Whoopi Goldberg, who plays a medium, is sitting at a table in a room surrounded by people in spirit arguing and trying to get through to loved ones. That is me on stage.

I have to be honest, at this point in my life and career, sometimes it annoys me that I still have to keep proving myself. It can get wearing. After all, I've been doing what I do for a very long time, and to keep having to justify myself can be trying. I also find it unfortunate that some mediums feel the need to demonstrate their ability by using dramatic effects and night-vision cameras, but on the whole I don't criticize anyone because, 'There but for the grace of God ...' as they say. I hope that by being myself and by being open I've helped a little bit in taking mediumship into the twenty-first century, but I'm not naive: I know there'll always be people who think I'm Paul Daniels! It would be so much easier if it *was* magic.

Ultimately, I'm a bubbly person; I've been told I have a big personality and, if people warm to that, it helps spirit too. There are no airs and graces to me, and I will always try to make my work entertaining, because spirit enjoys a show and a laugh as much as we do.

They respond so well to humour because they want us to know that they aren't sad. They want us to know that, although they are no longer with us, we mustn't be sad either, because one day we will all be together again.

PART TWO

On the Road

A Death in the Family

The clock was ticking down. One hour to go before show-time. Hair? Check. Make-up? Check. Everything was in place; now there was just the waiting. It was the calm before the storm and the last, vital bit of peace in which to compose myself before I strode out on to the stage and opened myself up to the afterlife. The buzz of the audience synchronized with the buzz of psychic energy in my head. The dressing room was quiet, but I could sense the expectation building up outside.

I wouldn't be human if I didn't get nervous; after all, I take a step into the unknown every night when I walk out on stage. I haven't a clue what will happen. I don't get any indication of what I'll see or hear. There's no script to learn when you're talking to the dead. There are no lines, and the only stage direction is 'enter stage right'. The rest is on a wing and a prayer. You have to have bucketloads of faith when you do what I do. You have to go with the flow and hope everything works out. Every now and then I stop and think to myself: what if it doesn't happen, what if the ability goes, what if one night I walk on stage and all I hear in my head is silence? After all, I'm not entirely sure why I have it, this ability that many people call a gift. I know it is a very special ability, I know it is precious and I believe it was given to me by someone or something. So if it was given, surely it can be taken away just as easily as it was granted. We joke sometimes, me and the crew: what would happen if, one night, the messages did mysteriously run dry? I tell them I'd finish the show with a sing-a-long, like an old-fashioned music-hall dame.

Thankfully, though, it hasn't failed me or the audience yet. We have a few hiccups along the way, but spirit wants to help, it's not there to trip me up, and 90 per cent of the time, what I see on stage ends up making sense to someone in the audience.

So, on this particular night, the venue was Wolverhampton, and I was quietly preparing myself in my dressing room.

It's a big crowd, Sal, I told myself. It was a sell-out: 1,200 bums on 1,200 seats.

In the hours leading up to the show, everything had been normal – if you can call the life of a medium normal, that is. John and I left the house early to drive from London to Wolverhampton. We assumed we'd miss the traffic but, of course, when we got to the outskirts of Birmingham, we realized that you never really miss the traffic in that part of the country because there is *always* traffic in Birmingham. John had driven us around the M25, up the M40 on to the M5 then on to the M6, where the traffic was chock-a-block.

Panicking that I'd be late, we had our usual bicker and I blamed John for bringing us on the wrong route. He hadn't, he'd just followed the sat nav, but you need someone to blame when you're stressed, and that's what husbands are for! We still arrived with plenty of time to spare; it's just that I like everything to run like clockwork. I'd get to the theatres in the morning for the evening shows if I could, but most of them don't even unlock their doors until mid-afternoon. This show was at the Grand Theatre; and it is. The five imposing arches that stretch across its façade contain a wealth of history. There's a lot of energy in those bricks and that mortar, which is good for my line of work. That residual force from years and years of use, all those thousands and thousands of people who walked through the doors and laughed and cried together, it all leaves a mark, like a stain on the fabric of the building. Mix that with the energy of the spirits waiting to contact their loved ones and you end up with a potent psychic soup. I reckon the residual energy in historic old buildings works like a lubricant and makes it easier for spirit to come through.

Now that we were here, backstage, I had unloaded my outfits and the bits and bobs I needed, just like I had done a hundred times before. Curlers, hair dryer, make-up, it was all laid out in front of me, and I went through the motions, readying myself for the show.

With the minutes passing, I was sitting peacefully in the dressing room, collecting my thoughts and finishing off a last cup of coffee before the start of the show. The psychic hum was all around me, a low-level electricity that was uniform and comforting, waiting expectantly for me to connect with the audience. No bad behaviour on this occasion. No spirits butting in, trying to make themselves known before it was time.

It was then that I felt it. A ripple. It's hard to explain in words, but imagine that the energy I was feeling that night was like the dead-calm surface of a pond. It was still and even, almost like a mirror. It's often like that before a show. Then, as the curtain call draws near, it builds up and

83

the surface starts to develop peaks and troughs. In the middle of really intense shows, those peaks and troughs become waves of energy, crashing around me. But this ripple was almost imperceptible, as if someone had just brushed the surface of the energy pond and created a tiny disturbance.

That's odd, I thought to myself. But it was such a fleeting feeling – a split second and it was gone – that I carried on preparing myself and didn't pay very much attention to it. Half an hour later, when my phone rang, I jumped.

You know the feeling you get late at night when the telephone rings and you're in bed – that feeling when you automatically know there is something wrong because people only call after bedtime in an emergency? It was like that. I knew there was a problem. And it wasn't just a question of me using my intuition. On a practical level, not many people know my personal telephone number. I can't give it out willy-nilly, not in my line of work. Heaven knows what kind of people I'd have calling me up. So only very close friends and family have my number. And most of them know when I'm working. So I knew that night that whoever was calling just a few minutes before I was due to go on stage must have something urgent to tell me.

Standing up to reach across for my phone, I saw the caller ID. It was my daughter Fern.

My heart began to beat fast in my chest. I picked up the trilling handset.

'Hello, love, what's wrong?' I could feel myself frowning.

Fern was crying on the other end of the line, her voice punctuated with sobs.

'It's Auntie Jean, Mum,' she said. 'She passed away this afternoon. You'll have to tell Dad.'

I stood open-mouthed. I felt like someone had hit me in the chest, taking all the air from my lungs. I didn't breathe. I grabbed the edge of the counter to steady myself and felt my legs buckle. My brain couldn't compute the information it had just been given.

Then the world and the implications of Fern's words came into sharp focus and I sucked in a lungful of air.

The tears came quickly. 'Not lovely Jean,' I cried. I was shaking now, and the tears were streaming down my face. My wonderful, kind sister-in-law Jean was dead. She and John were so close. He would be devastated. Then I thought of my husband. He was at the front of the theatre, at the merchandising stall, laughing and joking with the crew and customers, unaware that his life was about to crumple, unaware that grief was lurking just around the corner.

I deal with death every day but, when it affects me personally, my years of experience never make loss any easier. Ultimately, death can be cruel; it can snatch away those nearest and dearest to us in an instant. It doesn't matter that I knew Jean would be in a beautiful, peaceful place, that she would have finally been released from her years of suffering. That doesn't make loss any easier to bear because, suddenly, you realize that you won't see that person again for a long time. I knew there would be no more friendly phone calls and no more get-togethers where we'd be able to catch up with the gossip about each other's lives, because Jean's life was now over.

Colin, my production manager, walked into the dressing room.

I was standing, still with the phone in my hand, sobbing. My mascara was running down my cheeks like a dark slick.

'Sally! What's wrong, what's happened?' he gasped, walking over and hugging me.

I told him the tragic news, and he was adamant. 'Right, we'll have to cancel the show,' he said. 'There's no way you can go on stage after news like that.'

'There's no question,' I told him resolutely. 'There's an auditorium full of people out there who have all paid money to come here and see the show. I'm not going to let them down. The most important thing now is that John needs to know.'

'I'll tell him,' Colin offered.

'No, it has to come from me,' I insisted.

It was one of the hardest things I have ever had to do. John and Jean had always been close. He was very protective of her, not that she needed protecting. She was the life and soul. But, twenty years ago, she had been afflicted with a degenerative nerve disease. Slowly she'd been robbed of the use of her arms and legs and she'd ended up in a wheelchair, paralysed from the neck down. You'd understand anyone being bitter in that situation, but bitterness just wasn't in Jean. She wasn't one to feel sorry for herself and, despite her illness, she was always upbeat. She'd be on the phone for ages, laughing and joking. Her mind was as sharp as a knife. She followed my career and was always fascinated to know what I was up to. She read my books and watched the television shows. She especially enjoyed watching her brother and always chuckled at our onscreen tiffs and banter. She was a fan as well as family and a dear, dear friend. And now I had to tell John that she was gone.

Colin went to find him and brought him to the dressing room.

He knew as soon as he saw my tear-streaked face that something terrible had happened.

'What is it, love?' he asked, holding my arm.

'Oh, John, I'm so sorry. It's Jean . . .' My voice trailed off. I didn't have to say anything else.

'She's dead, isn't she?' he said, his eyes brimming with tears. We hugged, holding each other silently. When you've been married as long as John and I have, you don't always need words. We natter on and on about the little things in our lives but, when it comes to the big things, we can say more to each other with a hug than words can ever express. So we stood there for what seemed like hours, quietly comforting each other, sharing our energy.

'You know she would have wanted you to do the show,' John said quietly. I nodded.

'I know she's listening, John.' I addressed the air around us. 'Jean, darling, you are in a good place now, you are at peace, and I am so sorry but I have to go on and do this show.'

We both took deep breaths to steady ourselves. People were in their seats waiting. I'll cry after, I told myself. We hugged again and looked at each other, steeling ourselves to get through the following hours.

I know Jean would have been the first to say, 'Get out there, Sally, the show must go on.' There wasn't a selfish bone in that woman's body.

While I was on stage, John would have time to make the necessary phone calls. He told me afterwards that he was on autopilot for an hour, until the break, and it was only days later that he was able to think about how difficult it must have been for me to go out on stage. I was numb, but I had to compose myself. I had to get myself in the right frame of mind for the show. There was a theatreful of people looking forward to the psychic connection I was about to make. Then it struck me. *What if Jean comes through?* But she would never do something like that; she wouldn't interrupt the evening. She was too considerate to sabotage anything in that or any other way, and I couldn't let myself contact her either because I'd be in pieces; it would be too much for me.

That is one of my golden rules: I never turn my ability in on myself or towards family. I have to keep a divide between work and personal life. It's tough sometimes and often people fail to understand why I refuse to use my gift on a personal level, but if I started to look into my future and my family's future it would be like opening Pandora's box. It would lead to a whole heap of trouble.

'But surely you can see when bad things are going to happen and prevent them?' people say. But I don't believe in dabbling with my ability on that level. I think it would be dangerously irresponsible.

I believe that we all die when we are supposed to die, that the date is set and immovable. From the moment we take our first breath we are given a journey. We can deviate in certain areas but if we go off track too far we are always bought back to that pre-set route. Think of the people who survive accidents, seemingly by a miracle – people who go skydiving and their parachutes fail to open but they somehow survive the impact when they hit the ground, or the sole survivor in an airplane crash – they're not lucky; it just wasn't their day to die. It was not their time. Life is like a journey guided by sat nav. You have a start point and an end point and a route you are given. You have the freedom to deviate from that route if you want. You can turn when you are not advised to and the route will be recalculated for you and you will be given other options, but the end point is always the same.

And because I believe this is the way our destiny is shaped, I really do not want to know what will happen to me or the ones I love in the future. I don't want to know when any of us will die, because I know I cannot do a thing to change it and that knowledge will ruin the time I have left. You can't live if you have one eye on death. I have never even tried to see into my future. I doubt I would be able to anyway. I think this ability I have comes with a set of restrictions, and even thinking about turning it in on myself makes me feel very uneasy. I just push thoughts and feelings like that away. I don't get involved, and my family understands why.

I suppose when death impacts on my life on a personal level, it also has the possibility of impacting on my work. I don't get relatives trying to get through to me on stage and, if they did, I would have to put up the barrier. The show is not about me. And, ultimately, spirit is good and generous and pure. I feel they respect the boundaries I have had to draw. I look at my personal detachment as being similar to that of medical professionals who don't wish to treat their own families. I have to keep a professional distance, which seems weird when you are talking about death, but think of surgeons: many wouldn't want to operate on their own loved ones, would they?

So Jean didn't communicate with me that night, and I don't know how, but I got through it. I remember Julie coming into the dressing room during the interval to see how

I was, and I couldn't speak to her. I knew if I started to think about the situation, the floodgates would open. Strangely, as far as the show was concerned, it was an amazing night. Every message came through accurately and with clarity. The harmony between spirit and the audience seemed effortless. I like to think this was because spirit knew there was a new member of the Morgan clan in paradise that night and they knew how sensitive I was feeling so they put on an extra burst of energy and helped me.

I haven't tried to contact Jean in spirit for the reasons I've just mentioned, but I have once felt her watchful, guiding presence.

It was a year after her death, and John and I were taking a well-deserved holiday in the south of France. It was summer and the Côte d'Azur was glorious. We were staying in a friend's villa in the hills just outside Nice. At the beginning of the year I had undergone my gastric-bypass surgery and it had been an exhausting and gruelling six months. Unless you have had that type of procedure, it's hard to fathom just how life-changing it is. In essence, my surgeon gave me a whole new digestive system. But it was like the digestive system of a baby and, whereas before the op my stomach was used to consuming thousands of calories a day in breads and cakes and biscuits and snacks, this new pint-sized stomach could just about cope with soup in the early weeks. It took a long time and there were many unpleasant episodes before I was eating normal food again. I'll let you use your imagination to work out what those unpleasant episodes were – suffice to say, most of them involved me leaning over a toilet bowl!

The holiday was the first break I'd had since the operation. I'd shed almost 11 stone by that point, and had to keep pinching myself to make sure I wasn't dreaming and that I actually was wearing a swimming costume by the pool. John was by now thoroughly fed up with my squeals of delight every time I slipped on a pair of heels (remember: I hadn't worn them for thirty years) or slipped into a dress (ditto) or a strappy top (ditto). But you can't blame me. I was amazed by my new body. In short, life was good and I felt I had nothing at all to worry about.

It was a Wednesday, about halfway through the holiday, and John and I were relaxing in the sun. Fern, her husband Darren and their children, George and Max, were coming out to join us for the last few weeks of the break, so we were making the most of the peace and quiet. And as I sat there, not really thinking about anything, I felt her. I felt Jean, standing in the shade a little to my left under a palm tree that was softly swaying in the cooling breeze. I looked over, and there was no one there. It wasn't one of my seeing 'knowings'. She wasn't showing herself to me, but she was making sure I knew she was there.

It always surprises me when spirit is there and I'm not expecting it. Normally, I don't open myself up to it. I have learned to control that element of my ability over the years. In the early days, when I was a girl, spirit would just hijack my mind willy-nilly. Now I am much more in control. But maybe that day I was more relaxed than usual. I'd switched off. And there she was, in my mind, gently reminding me of her presence, looking after us. It wasn't a frightening feeling, not in the least. It was comforting and reassuring. And after a few seconds, she went, carried away on the warm Mediterranean breeze like an exotic butterfly.

I didn't tell John immediately, but later that evening over dinner I explained that I had felt his sister earlier in the day and wondered why she had chosen to let me know she was there at that particular time, so many months after her death.

The following day I got the answer. I received a call to do with an aspect of my business that needed urgent attention and was, at the time, very serious. There were a few problems that needed ironing out, and if they were not sorted there and then, they could have become much bigger. My peaceful holiday suddenly became very stressful. But we got through it and everything turned out well.

I realized that Jean had shown herself because she knew we were about to hit some of that turbulence life often has a habit of putting in the way of an otherwise smooth journey. Jean wanted to show herself just to say, 'Hey, things will get a bit rocky over the next few days, but everything will turn out fine. Don't worry.' She was there to offer her support. That is what spirits do. They might not always be apparent, they might just be a whisper on the wind or an unexpected thought at the back of your mind, but they are there watching over us, guiding us, protecting us. They are family, and family never dies.

Family Ties

In our lives, we forge thousands and thousands of relationships. From the cradle to the grave, we are constantly making contact with new people and forming friendships with our fellow human beings. From our first days in nursery, through to school, college, on to work, and in the clubs we join, the neighbourhoods we live in and the places we visit, there is a continual ebb and flow of people drifting in and out of our lives, a wave of humanity that we interact with. We are sociable creatures us humans. It is one of the things that sets us apart from other animals. The way we are with other people is what makes us human. When you actually sit down and think how many people we have relationships with during our lifetime, it's staggering. It is literally a cast of thousands – so many we can't possibly keep up with them all. Think of your Christmas card list: how many people are on that? Fifty maybe? A hundred? That is still a tiny percentage of the actual amount of friends most of us will make in a lifetime. And how many of those do you see on a regular basis? Not many, I reckon.

Of course, now there is social networking on internet sites such as Facebook. You can keep up with the daily thoughts and movements of people you hardly ever see. I've always thought how odd it is that you can find someone you went to school with, click a button and be accepted as their online friend, and then get a daily record of where they are, what they're thinking and what they're doing, even though you haven't spoken to them for twenty years and don't have any intention of speaking to them for the next twenty. They aren't proper friends, are they? These are disposable friendships. Kids nowadays collect them like they collected football cards in the old days. It's not the kind of friendship where you can call the other person up when you are miserable or pop round for a cuppa and a chat if you're feeling down. Those friendships are very rare and very valuable, the equivalent of a Gold card. They give you special privileges.

But if you go a rung above these kind of special friendships on the relationship ladder you get to the Platinum level – the top of the pile when it comes to the human relationships in our lives. You come to family, the indestructible unit that nurtures us through life and looks out for us, in most cases no matter what we do. Family are the people who, by and large, love us unconditionally. They are the ones who will always be there to support us through thick and thin, the ones we are bound to with a connection as strong as the toughest rope. They are the ones in life with whom we share a biological bond and, even if we are not blood relatives, we become so close to the people we share our day-to-day lives with that the link grows just as strongly as it would if we shared the same genes.

Our souls recognize this; our energy is attracted to the energy of the ones we love, in life and in death. It is magnetic, drawing us to our loved ones. Our loved ones in spirit hone in on our energy. It shines from us like a beacon, calling them to us. When we have a grandparent or someone we have lost in spirit, sometimes we think of them out of the blue. The thought of them pops into your head for no apparent reason. But, so many times, there is a reason. So many times, we summon them and their memory because there is something happening in life that we need support or advice with. We might not even realize it, but by thinking of them we are sending out a call for help, and they come. They come in many ways and many forms. They come to us in times of need, just like Jean did. They are the invisible guiding hands, helping us, holding us in times of trouble. We only have to think of them to make that connection. A thought of love sends a pulse of energy out from our souls into their realm, like a psychic text message. That is how we keep our loved ones alive on earth plane when they have passed.

I once heard someone say that we all die twice. Once when our bodies die, when we leave this life and go on to the next, and then again when someone says our name for the last time. It's a scary thought, isn't it? That one day there will be no one left on earth who remembers us (unless we've done something so massive and noteworthy our name is engraved in history). But I don't believe that we ever truly cease to be linked to this world. We have all made our mark here and we all leave family who go on to have family of their own. We all have those psychic energy connections that spread out like a spider's web and link to other energy patterns. The line goes on and, even if you don't know anything about your ancestry from generations back, they know about you and they are still linked to you.

I was shown an amazing example of how far back this link can go at a show one evening. It started, like so many readings, with names: two of them – Bill and Bob. But they were said not by one but by two different voices at the same time. It sounded in my head like voices coming through stereo headphones. The voices sounded almost identical but there was a very subtle difference between the two of them, a slight alteration in pitch: one voice was lower than the other. They were two separate spirits, but they were talking in harmony, almost as if with one voice.

'Twins,' I said out loud to the audience. 'I have two brothers here, they are in spirit and they are twins. They're giving me the names Bill and Bob.'

The connection works like a telephone line. Once it's made and I have linked to it, the data starts coming down the line. More information started to drop into my head. I was shown images. I saw the twins; they were men in their fifties or sixties. Around one I sensed trouble. I saw a caravan filled with junk and rubbish, I saw flies and sensed a dreadful stench that almost made me retch. Around the other man I saw order and peace.

I threw these details out to the audience and a hand shot up. An elderly man rose carefully to his feet. He was dressed in a checked shirt and cardigan and his salt-and-pepper hair was receding at the sides. He had other family with him, a woman who looked like she could be his sister and, possibly, a daughter. They all stood.

He explained that Bill and Bob were twins and had been his brothers.

Concerned about the disturbing images I was getting from one of the spirits, I asked gingerly, 'Was he found in a caravan?'

One of the women of the family explained that he had owned a caravan but they were unsure whether he died there. The rubbish and mess, she added, was because he was a hoarder. He had a compulsion to keep hold of things most of us would normally throw away.

In my mind's eye, I was being shown two distinct locations, and a huge distance between them.

'And were the twins estranged? Did they not get on?' I asked. 'They weren't estranged, but one lived here in the UK and the other lived in Australia, so they didn't see very much of each other,' the gentleman explained. 'And who is Florence?' I asked, as another name dropped into my head. 'There's somebody with them called Florence.'

'That's my grandmother on my father's side,' said the older woman.

So I had two generations in spirit now and two generations alive standing in front of me.

'This is turning into a proper family reunion, isn't it?' I laughed.

Another image dropped into my mind. It was a horse, a big grey with a white mane. Its nostrils were flared and I could see the whites of its eyes. I sensed danger.

'What's the link with horses?' I said. And as I did, almost on the periphery of the energy field I was tapped into, I felt another spirit materialize. He seemed older, more distant than the others. The best way to describe it is that we were having a conference call and this new caller who came on the line was phoning from a country far away, where the telephone system was not as advanced. It was a bad line, but I could just about pick him up, and I knew he had something to do with the horse.

I explained what I was feeling to the family in front of me, and the older lady gasped.

'My God,' she exclaimed. 'We looked into our family history a while ago and discovered that my mum's grandfather had died in a horse accident.'

'Bill and Bob are introducing your ancestors to you,' I said. 'They are showing you your family history.'

I was amazed. This woman's great-grandfather, whom she had never met, had been drawn to the theatre by the energy of his relatives, both living and dead.

Later, after the show, I thought about the implications of what had happened. Those people had been contacted by relatives they had never met or shared contact with. But the pull of their energy must have resonated with that man in spirit and his horse. Why else would he have come through? It dawned on me that every one of us has some form of family, even if we are estranged from the family we have on earth plane. We could feel totally alone in the world but we still all came from somewhere. We all have mothers and fathers, and they in turn had parents who had parents. We are linked back in time through our ancestors, and the energy we carry with us, our soul, is linked to spirit through ancestry. And it is because of this that no one ever dies alone. There is always someone there waiting to help you through to the other side.

They Never Leave Us

It's a lovely thought, isn't it? It's comforting to know that there will always be people looking out for us, that our families are helping us, even though we are not always aware that they are there. Just because they are no longer alive, it doesn't mean spirits cannot be useful. I think it is part of our basic human programming to want to help people. We are hard-wired to care – well, most of us are anyway. We all get a good feeling when we have helped others. I know personally that I have an inherent urge to help, especially when it comes to my family. And that instinct does not leave us when we pass.

It's touching to see how deep this urge goes. One of the most heart-melting times I saw a spirit help its earth-bound family happened in my own hallway at home.

It was a dark evening in November a few years ago and I was relaxing in the lounge at the back of the house watching telly – *Corrie*, probably, or one of the other soaps. John was in the front room watching football. I banish him there when there's a game on; he loves his football and has supported Fulham all his life. Personally, I can't see what the fuss is about and never watch it so, when there's a match on, I'm a football widow.

My office is opposite the front room where John watches his games, and when the front-room door is open the television reflects in the glass door of the office. From where I was sitting on the sofa in the back room, out of the corner of my eye, down the hallway, I could see the green of the football pitch reflected in the door.

That's when I saw him: a little boy in shorts who seemed to be reflected in the glass. It was just a flicker of an image on the edge of my vision as I was watching television. When I turned my gaze fully to the door, he was no longer there and the image had been replaced again by the reflection of the television and the football match.

That's odd, I thought. It must have been the adverts.

I carried on watching the TV in front of me but kept my attention fixed slightly to the periphery of my vision. I had a feeling that something strange was happening; it was as if my psychic antennae were being tweaked. And then, a few minutes later, the image of the boy reappeared, again in the corner of my eye. I could sense he was nervous, and I didn't want to startle him. Slowly, his head appeared, as if he was looking around a corner, and then he stepped out in full view. And as soon as I turned my head to look at the door of the office, he vanished and there was just the reflection of the game again.

'John,' I called. 'Is there a boy on the television down there?'

'What are you talking about? It's a game of football,' he called back.

'I know, but do they keep showing close-ups of a little boy?'

By now John was laughing.

'No, why would they do that?'

'I don't know, but I keep seeing the reflection of a little boy in the glass of the office door.'

'Have you been drinking?' John joked.

I knew what I had seen, and the only thing I'd been drinking was a cup of tea. The boy was about six or seven, he had a mop of dark hair and was dressed in a T-shirt and a pair of three-quarter-length trousers.

By now I knew it wasn't a reflection and sensed that there was an energy in the doorway of the office. All houses that have been lived in contain residual energy of the lives that have been played out inside them. And not just humans but even animals. In our house, we have spirits that I tune into; they're like faded photographs that have been laid over the top of space and time. You'll think I'm mad, but there is even the ghost of a mouse in the back room. When we were renovating the house we had to knock through a chimney breast and behind the fireplace we took out there were mice, so we put down traps. I hate killing anything, but mice are pests and we had to get rid of them because, once they start breeding, you have a problem on your hands. We got rid of the mice but one of them must have really liked living in the house because, a few weeks after the work was completed, I was sitting there watching the telly and I suddenly jumped and screamed when I saw something scurry across the floor. Only this wasn't a mouse, it was a ghost mouse. It is still there. Every now and then I see it scuttling about. I've got used to it now, but it always makes me feel so guilty, because I was the one who put the trap down that killed it. Anyway, my point is that this boy was not part of the psychic fabric of the house that I was used to, so I knew that he must have appeared for a reason, because when spirits show themselves to us and contact us it is always for a reason.

Sometimes they are drawn because they feel that family link; at other times it's to offer support or a warning.

I walked down the hallway slowly. I didn't want to startle the boy; he had seemed so nervous. John looked up from the match, saw me creeping along like a cat burglar and rolled his eyes. I got to the office and peeked carefully round the door. Nothing. There was no sign of the boy, but I could feel his energy. He was in the room; I could feel a stillness around him. The light was off, and the room was illuminated by the grey-white glare of my computer screen.

Because of my work, the computer is on constantly. I try to switch it off in the evenings if I'm at home, but there will always be something that needs attending to or an email that needs answering, and it's easier to leave it on stand-by than to keep turning it on and off. I don't know why but, at that moment on that night, my intuition told me to click on the email inbox. At the top of the list my attention was immediately drawn to an unopened message from a man with an Italian-sounding name. I opened it and gasped.

The message was so sad. It came from a doctor who lived in Milan. He had heard about my work, and it had taken him weeks to find my contact details. In his email he explained that, three weeks ago, his son had fallen ill and, after a very brief illness, had died. Understandably, both he and his wife were devastated, but his wife was so distraught she could no longer function. She was bedbound with grief, unable to eat or sleep, and he feared for her health. He was desperate for me to make contact with him and speak to his wife in the hope that maybe I could offer her some comfort and reassurance that their beloved son was at peace in the afterlife. I knew as I read down the email that the little boy who had shown himself in my house was their son and that he was so worried about his mummy that he needed to show himself to me so I could tell her he lived on. He had an instinct to help her and to care for her in death in the same way she had cared for him in life. I called the man that night and spoke to his wife and told her exactly what had happened. She sobbed uncontrollably on the phone and, over the following weeks, we stayed in contact. The grief never left her, it never does, but knowing that her little boy was in spirit and in Heaven gave her the strength to carry on.

There is something very comforting about knowing that spirits care and look out for their families. And it's not just the big things they worry about. They come through at my shows for some pretty strange reasons.

I'll always remember one spirit, Derek. I laugh now when I think of him. How could anyone forget Derek?

He came through loud and clear at a show I was doing in the south of England. Derek didn't need an invitation. Bang! He was there, and his energy was so strong I found myself overtaken by his mannerisms. He was gruff and outspoken. It was like being possessed by Alf Garnet.

I found myself, hands on hips, repeating his words to the audience.

'My name's Derek,' I said in the loud, deep voice that belonged to him. 'Lynne?' I boomed. There was a gasp from the audience as two attractive women stood up. They knew straight away who had come through.

''Ere, I'm only 'ere, what's all this about then?' I said, in Derek's voice. He wanted the girls to know he was there.

The audience laughed. One of the girls explained that her name was Linda, her middle name was Lynne and Derek was their father.

'Debbie!' I said. The other lady shrieked. 'I was watching you, you'll lose that black purse.'

The other girl, Debbie, nodded. They were dumbfounded. Their dad had come through to warn them to be careful not to lose a purse. But that's what us parents do, isn't it? We fuss over the tiniest things because we care. And, for Derek, it wasn't the content of the message that mattered as much as making contact in the first place. Like most spirits, he wanted his family to know he was still around them.

I found out later that the way I was striding about on stage and the tone of my voice were exactly the mannerisms of dear old Derek. I'm not aware of taking on the form of spirits but, since doing the live shows, I feel much more of the person who is spirit. Believe me, I'd sometimes rather that wasn't the case. I'd rather not be stomping around, bellowing out messages in a gruff Cockney accent, but that's just the way it happens. And it makes for a deeper connection for the receivers and gives the rest of the audience a good laugh too.

Then Derek showed me a man smoking a cigarette, except it wasn't a normal cigarette. It was a cannabis joint. Let me just say, for the record, that I've never taken drugs but I haven't lived the life of a nun either. I've been around people smoking pot and I know what a joint looks like. And Derek was showing me a joint.

I mimed what I was seeing and told the girls what Derek was warning them about. 'He can get rid of that stuff,' I said. They laughed nervously.

Then Derek turned his attention to his daughters' shoe fixations.

'What you doing with all those shoes?' he asked. They laughed and admitted they both had far too many. 'They stink,' he told them.

Although Derek was a character, loud and boorish, I could also feel a huge warmth coming off his energy. He loved the fact that he had shocked his girls by coming through, but I could feel nothing but love.

'Nothing's going happen to you while I'm ' ere,' he told them. 'I'm watching the pair of you.'

Then he gave me the name Alan.

'Who's Alan?' I asked.

'That's Mum's boyfriend,' they answered.

'Ooops,' I said. 'He doesn't like that.' And then he explained that he had never kissed his wife the way Alan kisses her.

'We don't want to know this,' laughed the girls. Then I sensed another energy with Derek, a young man or teenager. I was given the name Luke.

I sensed that Derek was a father-figure someone who in life liked to look after people. I asked the women standing up if they knew a Luke in spirit. They didn't. But they were with Debbie's daughter, who tugged at her mum and stood up.

'My boyfriend's friend Luke passed a few months ago,' she said.

'He's here, love,' I told her as she began to cry. I was given an image, not a nice one, but I get given these messages for a reason and always relay faithfully what I get, even at the risk of upsetting the person the message is for.

Spirits are not here to upset or unsettle us, they show us things for proof.

'Did he break his nose?' I asked the girl. 'His nose is flat against his face.' She confirmed that Luke had died in a motorbike accident.

It was obviously a terrible accident and Luke had sustained horrible facial injuries and this bothered him. Not because spirit is vain, far from it. When we die, we leave our bodies behind. They are just vessels for the soul. But what troubled Luke was knowing that his mother had been upset by the details of the accident.

He gave me a message to give to the daughter.

'He didn't like the way he looked. He says, "You have to tell my mum I'm sorry,"' I told her. 'Your granddad is looking after him.'

From warning about lost purses to commenting on foot hygiene and introducing the spirit of a friend who wanted to reassure his grieving mother, Derek certainly made the most of his brief few minutes in the spotlight!

Of course, they're not always as funny as Derek. But one thing all psychic family connections have is love. Sometimes the feelings of love and tenderness that flood through me when I connect a living person with their relatives in spirit are so strong they bring me to tears.

The pull from a spirit can be overwhelming. That pull is often strongest during my shows when I reach into the basket of photographs that audience members leave. To the untrained eye, it looks like a totally random act. And for me it is. I have no idea what I'm going to pull out when I reach into my little wicker basket. I don't see what goes into it or who puts photographs in it. But I do feel the pull of energy when I reach in. Spirit directs me, it guides me to pick the right picture, usually with amazing results.

At one show, I pulled out a tiny black-and-white passport-sized photograph of an attractive woman in her early thirties with dark, permed hair. Judging by the hairstyle and her clothes, the photo was taken in the eighties. I held it up to the camera on the stage, and the image was shown on the screen behind me.

'If this is your photo, can you stand up, please?' I asked the audience.

A young girl, perhaps in her early twenties, stood up. The family resemblance was unmistakable. She had the same soft features and dark hair as the lady in the picture.

I felt a warm surge of energy as the connection was made. I was immediately given the name Rita, or Anita.

I asked the girl if these meant anything to her, and she replied that the lady in the photograph had an auntie called Rita who had passed.

'She is with her,' I told the girl. 'She's with her aunt, they are together.' I knew instinctively that the woman in the picture was her mother. And the first thing she wanted her daughter to know was that she was not alone. Spirits loved to reassure us. They have an urge to let us know that they are released from any pain they suffered in life and are in a place of happiness and peace.

I could hear the woman in spirit talking in calm, loving tones about her softly spoken, shy daughter.

'Your mum is so proud of you,' I told her. The girl began to cry, and the emotion was tangible. You could have reached out and touched the love between mother and daughter, it was that strong. You could have heard a pin drop in the theatre then. I felt tears well in my eyes and the spirit showed me the details of her last months alive.

I felt a wave of exhaustion wash over me, making me drowsy.

'She says to me, "I was so tired. I couldn't move, how could I live like that? I couldn't even lift my arm,"' I explained to the young woman. 'Your mum, she loved life, she loved you with a passion that you could only imagine.'

The girl tearfully explained that her mum had contracted a virus that attacked her spinal cord and left her paralysed from the waist down.

Her mum showed me moving snatches of their life together. She showed me them shopping for clothes and giggling like friends; she showed me how her daughter had cared tenderly for her as her illness progressed.

'She says, "You tickled my toes,"' I told the girl as an image dropped into my mind. In it the girl was sitting at the foot of her mother's sickbed, gently kneading and massaging her feet.

'She says, "I hope you know how grateful I was,"' I added. The girl confirmed that, as her mother lay stricken, unable to move, she had developed bed sores and suffered increasingly dry skin. Concerned, the caring daughter would regularly massage her mother and rub skincream over her body to try to ease the pain and help with the sores.

By now there was not a dry eye in the auditorium.

Then a name flashed into my mind.

'Who is Sarah?' I asked.

'That's me,' replied the girl. The connection was so strong that the accuracy was incredible. My senses were zinging. My nostrils filled with a sweet scent.

'You will smell your mum, because she tells me you used to put perfume on her.'

The girl, Sarah, nodded.

'You will smell her perfume,' I told her. 'Remember what I said: she loves you more than you can ever imagine.'

The saddest part of such an emotional reading is moving on, but they all have to come to an end and, after such an amazing connection, the girl was elated and explained that the accuracy of the reading had given her hope and comfort.

No One Dies Alone

Reading for people is not always just about putting them in touch with departed loved ones and passing on messages of love. It's not always about helping people with their grief. Everyone has different motivations for coming to see a medium, and some of them are more subtle than others. Some people come to us to tap into our heightened sense of intuitiveness. They want answers or they want guidance. Many women come for advice about relationships. More women come than men, but that doesn't mean that, once they are with a medium, men are any less sensitive than women when it comes to expressing their emotions. I always think it's lovely when a family man comes and sees me, because he is being man enough to say, 'Help me.' Men are not naturally emotional creatures, because they often feel the need to be strong, whether in their relationships with family, with their wives and partners, or in work or with their friends. It's all about being macho.

I find I'm gentler with men. I make even more of an effort to make them feel comfortable and maybe treat them with kid gloves for a while, because I appreciate how alien it is for many fellas to sit and talk about personal and private aspects of their lives. That's where my personality helps. I'm like a comfortable aunt or a gran or a mum. It's an amazing compliment that, so often, men come up to me after a show or hijack me when I'm shopping and say,

'You're just like my mum,' or, 'I wish you were my mum.' It's just something that's there in my personality, a natural nurturing instinct. I've been like it ever since I can remember. When I was younger, people used to say to me, 'I wish you were my sister.'

Although men come for different reasons to women, it's always gratifying to help and to see them open up and accept spirit. Often they want answers to family questions that may have been bugging them for years. Men are like that, you know. They won't admit it, but they hate not having all the answers, and they love gossip even more than women.

All families have secrets, and more and more people are becoming obsessed with uncovering the details of their ancestry. I think it must be because of the popularity of television shows such as *Who Do You Think You Are?* and family-tree websites. Nowadays, researching family history is a hobby for a lot of people, and when you hit a brick wall and can't find the answers, who better to call than a medium? In one recent reading I was asked to find out whether my client had been adopted. She had always felt that she didn't quite fit in with the rest of her family and was suspicious because there were no photographs of her as a baby. Her suspicions had driven her family apart after her father died, and she also wanted reassurance from him that he understood why she had her doubts and did not blame her for dividing the family.

I also got to play psychic detective a few years ago when a man came to see me to clear up some questions that had been troubling his mother for many years. She wanted to know more about why her mother walked out on her when she was a little girl.

When he sat in front of me, I immediately felt his maternal grandparents. He explained that his grandmother had walked out on his mother when she was just five and they had never been able to trace her after that.

'I know the reason why your grandmother wasn't around your mother,' I told him as the details were fed to me from spirit. 'She was banished.'

He nodded.

'I think your mother's mother had a relationship with someone,' I continued. 'Your grandmother had shoes with a tiny heel on them, and when she was banished from the home she left them behind, like she left everything behind. She went just with the clothes she was wearing. And your mum would play with those shoes; she wore them in dressing-up games.'

An image flashed into my head. I saw a little girl holding a card. There was a hand-drawn picture on the front of it depicting a pretty bunch of violets. As the girl began to read the words inside the card it was violently snatched away from her.

It was one of those random examples of images that appear to me as if by osmosis, and I recounted faithfully to the man what I was picking up. He confirmed that that had indeed happened. His mother had received a card which she suspected was from her mother, but feelings obviously ran so deep in the household that it was taken from her before she could read it.

'It was from her mother for her birthday,' I told him.

'I believe your mother's mother has passed over,' I told him sadly. He nodded.

I can't always tell people what they want to hear. I'm

sure he would have loved to hear that his gran was alive somewhere, but I can only give what I get and sometimes closure doesn't come in the form we would hope for.

Death is always sad, whether it is a death we are prepared for and know about or whether we hear it second hand about someone we hardly know. When it's a death in the family, it always affects us.

The raw grief I see in the people I read for never fails to humble me. People are so brave, picking up their lives and battling on through grief.

I read for a lovely lady not so long ago, and her bravery was amazing. She had lost her beloved father just a few months before the reading, and it was obvious she was struggling to come to terms with her loss.

Dressed in black with pulled-back hair, she melted into tears when I told her I had her father with me in spirit.

I knew exactly how strong the link between them was because, before I even set eyes on her, I could feel his energy. I could feel his anticipation. She sat dabbing her eyes with a tissue as I told her that the first thing I was picking up was a feeling that someone had a problem with their hair, as if they were losing it. She nodded quietly as I went on to tell her that I was being shown a map of America in my mind.

'I'm planning on moving there next year,' she explained.

She showed me a photo of her father, standing proud and smiling in a wedding suit.

Words tumbled into my mind.

'I like to talk and I couldn't talk,' I said softly, relaying the words that were being placed in my mouth. 'I never had the energy to get the words out.'

'He couldn't speak properly. He was paralysed,' she confirmed through sobs.

I saw an airport in my mind, and the lady explained that her father travelled a lot and had a deep-vein thrombosis that triggered a stroke when he was on a plane flying to South Korea. The flight lasted another ten hours and, by the time the plane landed at its destination, there was very little hope for him.

'He says to me, "My dad visited me, my dad came, and when I saw him I knew it was time to go."'

Then she told me the significance of the hair I had been shown at the start of the reading. The last time she spoke to her father, she was in the hospital in Korea with him and he was being wheeled to theatre for a five-hour brain operation. He said to her, 'They're Australians, these people.' She assumed he was confused because of the stroke and assured him that he was in Korea, not Australia. But smiling through a half-paralysed mouth, he pointed to his head, which had been shaved for the operation, and said, 'No, they're Australians, they're sheep shearers.' They were the last words he said, and they made her laugh. That was six months before she came to see me, and she had not laughed since. But she walked out of the reading with a smile on her face and now had no doubt her father was in Heaven with people who loved him.

We never really let our family go. The bond is too strong. And after they pass, most of us mark their passing and remember them more than we even realize. In some cultures, the dead never really leave the family home. In the Far East, in countries such as Vietnam, a place in the house is put aside for the family to erect a shrine to their dead relatives. They honour them every day with offerings and incense and even leave food out for them. And whenever there is family news, like a birth or a wedding, the dead relatives are always the first to know. It's customary to go to the shrine and fill them in on the family gossip. I suppose it's the same as visiting a grave or having someone's ashes on the mantelpiece.

Many people ask me for advice on what they should do with a loved one's remains. Well, there are so many options. You can keep them at home, scatter them in the person's favourite place, share them out among family members so everyone has something of the person who has passed – or you can always go for one of the more extreme options. Honouring the remains of the dead is becoming big business. You can have remains flown into space, or exploded in a firework; you can have them crushed into a diamond or hand-blown into a glass vase. You can even have them turned into paint or crunched into a fine sand and placed inside an hourglass. If you ask me, there is nothing better than getting a nice pot in the garden, putting the ashes inside that and planting a tree or a rose bush in it.

But really, whatever we do with the remains of our loved ones, we carry our relatives with us wherever we go. They are in our hearts always, pulsing in tune with our spiritual energy, waiting for the day our energy is released through the natural process of death, and on that day they can come and join with us and take us into the afterlife.

Suffer Little Children

I knew she was harbouring a huge weight before she even spoke. She sat quietly in the front room waiting for me to finish the reading. Even John, at his most chirpy, couldn't persuade her to have a cup of tea and a natter. She was distant and detached, as if her mind was locked away somewhere dark and bleak.

She had pale-grey skin and looked as if she hadn't slept in months. Her sad, sad eyes were sunken in dark circles. Her dark hair was scraped back in a bun and she wore a long black coat that she refused to take off. For the sake of client confidentiality, I'll call her Emma. She was in her early thirties but looked an age older, as if the weight of the world had dragged the life from her.

She had driven up from Brighton after making an appointment the previous week. She didn't say why she was coming; clients rarely do. They need to keep their reasons from me, I understand that. When I get it correct, when spirit floods in and tells me its secrets, it gives the client validation. They know I am genuine. The accuracy feeds trust and lets them know that I do what I say I do and that the reading is not some sort of magic trick. Most of the time, the only thing I know about new clients is their first name.

Emma had come to me on the recommendation of a friend. Even before I first laid eyes on her I felt a chill around her. As I walked from my office across the hallway into the front room to greet her, I felt a change in temperature.

'Come in, love,' I ushered as I walked into the front room to introduce myself. She looked such a sad, drawn little thing, my heart immediately went out to her.

She tried to smile and stood slowly, offering her hand for me to shake. But the expression on her face came out all wrong. It looked like a face that had forgotten how to be happy.

Shaking her hand before we sat down to talk, I felt the weight of sadness that hung over her like that coat: draped heavily over her shoulders, pulling her down to the deepest recesses of despair which, thankfully, most of us will never have to experience. This was a woman in trouble. A woman so infected by grief it was altering her body and mind. She had lost the will to live.

That happens in the most extreme cases. People just cannot see a way through, they cannot see a light at the end of the tunnel, and they believe they would be better off dead.

It's a different process to that which leads to suicide; there is no conscious planning. Desperate people such as Emma don't go and buy a rope and write a final letter of explanation. No, people like Emma just decide subconsciously not to bother living any more. And then they wait for nature to take its course.

As we stepped into my office and sat down for the reading, I felt him, and suddenly everything clicked into place. He was a child, a small boy around four years of age. He was Emma's son, he was in spirit and he wanted his mummy.

I drew in a deep breath. Taking her hand and looking her in the eye as tenderly as I could, I said, 'I have him here, darling, he's right there at your side.'

It was as if the sheet of ice that had kept her face fixed had suddenly melted. The detached, brave façade fell away and Emma's face twisted into a tortured expression of anguish.

'Is he in pain?' she managed through strangled sobs.

'He's in a wonderful place, he's in Heaven. He loves his mummy so much,' I told her.

She crumpled in the chair, overcome.

I could see the little boy in my mind's eye. He had big, brown, mischievous eyes and was standing in a kitchen. There was a fridge in the background and fixed to it with magnets was a child's painting. It was of a house and three brightly coloured stick people: the boy, his mummy and his daddy. On the floor there was an upended saucepan, and steaming white liquid was split over the linoleum flooring. As I focused on the scene, what looked like a huge angry red birthmark appeared on the boy, running down the back of his neck and across his shoulders. He began to scream. And then I felt a hot jolt that made me jump in my seat.

'It burns, Mummy,' I said, repeating the words I was hearing.

Emma nodded, and I could feel an overwhelming sense of guilt coming from her.

'It was an accident,' I told her. 'It wasn't your fault; he knows that. He doesn't blame you, he never has and he never will.'

She hung her head and filled the room with wracking sobs.

I saw it all then. Her little boy showed me everything.

Up until two months ago, she had lived the dream. She lived in a lovely house by the sea in Brighton, she had a part-time job working with disadvantaged children, she had a loving husband who worked in finance and she had her son, Josh, whom she idolized. He was a fun-loving, outgoing child, full of laughter, and inquisitive about the world around him, like all boys his age.

One day Emma was making him his favourite drink, hot chocolate. But being the super mum she was, she was doing it the proper way, not heating up an instant drink in the microwave but warming the milk on the hob first before stirring the powdered cocoa into the pan. For just a split second she walked to the other side of the kitchen to get the sugar, and Josh, who was excited about what was going on above him, reached up and pulled the handle.

The steaming milk tipped down his neck and scalded him. Because of the training Emma had been given in her job she knew she needed to get cold water on her son and took him to the bathroom, where she gently tried to ease his pain and calm his agonized screaming. She called for an ambulance and, frantic with worry, accompanied Josh to the hospital when it arrived.

The burn was bad. It was a third-degree burn down the back of his neck and across his shoulders. Josh was in agony and needed to be sedated. The skin had blistered off his shoulders and he couldn't lie on his back to sleep as the injury was too painful. Doctors warned Emma that her son would need skin grafts as the wound healed. No one ever mentioned that he may die and, as the days went on, the immediate danger began to subside. Slowly, Josh's angry wound appeared to start to heal and after several days in hospital under close observation, he was allowed to go home. The panic and fear wore off. Several times a day, Emma carefully applied lotion to Josh's injury, all the time fighting the awful feeling of guilt that infected her heart. Was it her fault? Why had she taken her eyes off him, even if it was just for a split second? Of course, accidents like that can happen to anyone, but that was no comfort for Emma.

Then, three weeks after the accident, as Emma and Josh were finally getting over the mental scars and the doctors were planning what further surgery Josh would need, he developed a temperature.

Emma thought he was coming down with flu but, after a few hours and some Calpol, his temperature continued to rise and he became listless and weak. She rushed him to hospital and, after an anxious hour of tests, doctors diagnosed blood poisoning. Somehow, despite Emma's diligent and loving care, bacteria had entered his body through the still-open wound.

Josh fought for days but his condition continued to deteriorate. Weakened already by the shock of the initial accident, he was finding it harder and harder to beat back the poison in his veins. Emma kept vigil by his side. When doctors put him in an induced coma to try to help him, she sat by his side, reading his favourite stories and stroking his pale skin. But the infection was too strong. One by one, Josh's organs began to fail. After four days in intensive care, Emma was given the crushing news: 'Your son is brain dead. He will never recover.'

She made the agonizing decision to turn off the machine

that was breathing for him and sat in shock, repeating the words, 'I'm so sorry,' in her son's ear as the last breath of air left his lifeless lungs and he slowly ebbed away.

The grief and guilt she felt had become so raw it was eating away at her like a cancer. It had infected every part of her life. Most days she could barely get out of bed. She couldn't see any reason to carry on. Her relationship with her husband was suffering terribly, because she believed she deserved to be punished. She blamed herself entirely. The guilt ate away at her from morning to night, she hadn't been to work since the accident and in her mind she didn't care if she never got out of bed again. In desperation, a friend who happened to have had a reading with me several years ago advised her to make a booking. Even her husband, a cynic, encouraged it. They felt that anything that might offer her a glimmer of hope would be worthwhile.

And so there she sat, directly in front of me, the shattered shell of a once happy and fulfilled human being. However, just me telling her what I was seeing confirmed to her that there was a force of nature beyond what we perceive, and although there was no way in the world one reading could ever help relieve the feelings of hopelessness and anguish she was suffering, simply by giving her the details I was getting from spirit – the name Josh, the details of his injury and the weeks following it and, most importantly, the message from him that cried out, 'Mummy, it's not your fault. You cannot blame yourself' – she began to see that perhaps she might be able to live with her grief, rather than be overwhelmed by it. She began to see that maybe there is a life after death and that, because of that, death does not mean the end. She began to feel a tiny bit of hope and, in the sea of despair she had been lost in for so many weeks, that sliver of hope was the lifeline that would keep her afloat.

Emma continued to come and see me and, each time, Josh would come through. You couldn't keep him away. She worked through a lot of her darkest thoughts and feelings with me and, each session, as Josh's energy connected with his mum's and he gave me more and more information about their life together, she slowly started to have faith: faith in an afterlife, and faith that her son was still around her and at peace, that he was in a good place. She also began to start to forgive herself – not that she had done anything wrong. Thanks to his constant messages of love, she started to realize that, tragically, accidents happen, and often they cannot be avoided. Her relationship with her husband improved and she started to open up and let him support her. He had been in turmoil too. She had lost a son, and so had he; she was not the only one to be bereaved. They worked through their pain as a couple, and she also went back to work. She started living again.

Of course, in the face of such tragedy, it would be glib of me to say that Emma got over her son's death. Of course she didn't. How could she? There were plenty of days when she felt just as hopeless and anguished as she had felt in her darkest times. There probably still are. Child deaths are not something that parents can ever heal from. The scars stay for ever and can be just as raw years, even decades, after the death. No, Emma still had a lifetime of sorrow ahead of her, but the difference was that she had begun to see that she could move on, that there was hope.

In one of the last meetings we had I was shown something that I had to be very careful about sharing with her. I never withhold the messages I am given, because I know I am given them for a reason, but sometimes they seem inappropriate, and Sally the medium has to defer to Sally the human, the mother and grandmother. With Emma, I was shown a little baby. I was shown an image of her, her husband and a little baby son. I knew it meant that, within the next year, she would be pregnant. But you have to be so considerate when you give news like that to someone who has lost a child. If you aren't careful, it can come out sounding as if you are saying, 'Don't worry. Have another child; it'll replace the one you have lost.' Anyone who has lost even a dog will know what I mean. If you lose a dog, so many people say, 'Get another one.' But life doesn't replace life.

So I gently told Emma what I was being shown, and she genuinely seemed pleased. Two weeks later, I saw her for what I thought would be the last time.

However, there is a postscript to this story. About a year after that last appointment, there was an unexpected knock on the door. It was a weekend in March, and John answered. I heard voices in the hallway, and John called me. I didn't recognize who it was at first. There was a tall man and a tanned woman in a dress holding a small bundle.

'It's Emma and her husband,' said John. 'They were just passing, and they wanted to pop in and say hello.'

At first it didn't register who this Emma was. But then the penny dropped. She looked so much happier and younger than the last time I had seen her that she was unrecognizable.

I screamed.

'You were right,' she smiled, holding the bundle towards me.

I took it and stared inside the white blanket at a pair of mischievous, wide brown eyes that looked strangely familiar.

I looked back at Emma, and she mouthed the words, 'Thank you.'

The Hardest Death of All

It's always very obvious when a child comes through. There's a distinct difference in both the spirit and the receiver of the message. I know immediately from that first connection, that first feeling, that there is a child in spirit. Children are different, they're a gift from God; they're as special in life as they are in death. Perhaps it's because I'm a mum and a grandmother, but the children really affect me. I can't help it; I'm human, after all.

It's hard to explain, but the spirit of a child feels different to that of an adult. I can sense the innocence. In the receiver I can sense the injustice and the pain. Whenever I am dealing with a child death, there is always a sense of unfairness. 'Why did my child have to die?' It is a question I'm asked again and again. Child deaths, especially the really unexpected ones, are the times when faith gets tested to its absolute limit. There are so many emotions swirling around these readings it gets hard to concentrate. There is a grief so raw it is overwhelming and, as with Emma, there is usually guilt. Even if there is nothing the parents could have done to prevent the death, they will still feel guilt. They will spend years agonizing: 'Why wasn't I there? Why couldn't I have done more?' I remember reading once about the guilt felt by the father of little toddler James Bulger. James was murdered by two children in Liverpool in 1993 after being abducted from a shopping centre. His father was not there and could never have prevented the awful tragedy that befell his little son but he said afterwards how he was always haunted by the thought that James must have been crying for him and must have wanted his daddy to come and protect him and save him. And the guilt ate away at him. That is such a common thought process when a child dies. Even if a child dies of illness, a parent will always wonder whether they could have done anything differently, whether they could have gone to a doctor earlier or noticed the symptoms sooner. More often than not I'm brought to tears when a little 'un comes through and connects with its mummy or daddy.

You see, children lose none of their personality in death. Their energy is childlike: it can be light and playful; it can be mischievous and naughty. And then you get the ones who are crying.

Sadness does not exist in spirit, but often a child will mirror what they felt as they passed to help me identify them to their parents. And that feeling of a child in spirit crying out for its mummy or daddy can be overwhelming. I have to say to myself, 'Sally, this is the job you have chosen,' otherwise I would give up.

It's not a burden, though, and when I get readings like this, the ones that really affect me, I have to be philosophical about my ability. I have to look at it as a blessing that I am able to bring comfort and solace to people at very difficult times of their lives, no matter how hard it can be at the time.

Sometimes those words and sentiments I deliver from beyond the grave will be the most important and profound words the people I am delivering them to will ever hear. They will be the reassurance a grief-stricken mother or father has been looking for. The content of the message is not necessarily important. It doesn't have to be a profound statement; that is not what spirits usually deliver, especially children. A child isn't going to come through with some poignant message about the afterlife, it's more likely to come through with a simple message of love and innocence. The most important thing is that the grieving parent knows that the message they are receiving is from their child. Their certainty that the message is from their child is what counts, because that is what gives the mum or dad the knowledge that their child is in a good place and is no longer suffering.

I've mentioned before that I have to be faithful to the messages I am asked to deliver, that I deliver them literally, I say exactly what I'm seeing and hearing, but with children in spirit I am always more sensitive in the way I deliver the message. I don't choose what I am asked to say but I can choose the way I pass it on. Child death is such a terribly sensitive area, and whenever a bereaved mother comes to me my heart aches for her. Even though I feel their emotions and see their pain, and even though I have felt the loss of a child on one level myself, I still can't begin to fathom what it must feel like when your son or daughter dies. I've got nothing but admiration for the bereaved mums and dads who come to my shows, because I suspect that, if it were me, I would never be able to pick myself up and function. When I'm dealing with someone and talking about the death of a child, I always empathize with them. Even if it's an eighty-year-old woman who has lost a sixty-year-old child, she has still lost her child. I make sure that madcap Sally the entertainer is kept firmly in her box and am calmer, sympathetic and as compassionate as possible.

Whenever I'm doing a show and a child comes through and a hand in the audience goes up, I am awestruck. I think it is testament to just how strong people can be that they can stand there in a theatre full of people and talk to me about the tragedies they have suffered. The fact that these parents can stand there and listen to me, and that they are nice to me and polite and thankful for the messages I am giving them blows me away. Hopefully they get comfort and validation from what I do. In fact, when I get home at the end of day and sit and reflect on what I have done, the times when I have helped bereaved parents are the times when I am most proud of my work. To be able to go out and bring hope to people who have lost all hope is a real honour. I wouldn't go as far as to say that I bring closure. I don't know if I'd use that term because, when it comes to child bereavement in particular, I don't think you ever get closure. I have read for people who lost children decades previously, but they still feel that sadness. It becomes a part of them, like a piece of shrapnel buried in their hearts that never leaves and, sometimes, without warning, starts to ache. No, I like the term 'hope'. If I can give that person hope, they can carry on and will live with the knowledge that, one day, they will be reunited with the soul of their child. Even if that hope lasts just for one moment, it's worth it. In my shows, I know the people who receive the messages will leave the theatre and then may be influenced by doubters, but at least just for a few minutes they have made that connection and have been given that glimpse into the afterlife. When I get feedback from readings that involve children and I hear how parents have benefited, I know what I'm doing is important.

One of the most powerful experiences I had with the spirit of a child was at a show in Norwich a few years ago. It's one of those readings that will always stay with me. It was possibly one of most heart-rending and memorable ones I have ever done. And whenever I ask the crew who come on the road with me what their most memorable reading is they will always say the same name: 'Ellie.'

The Girl Who Sings on the Stairs

Wasn't it Forrest Gump who said, 'Life is like a box of chocolates: you never know what you're going to get?' Well, death is like that too. When I'm standing in the wings, waiting for the fanfare to die down before I step out on stage and start my shows, I have no idea who is in the audience and what is waiting for me in spirit. I might have felt and heard and seen little snatches of messages and voices, but I don't know how it will all fit together.

That's one of the exciting things about my work: you never know what you'll get; you don't know if it will be a hard centre or a soft centre, dark chocolate or milk chocolate.

The night Ellie came through I was performing in Norwich. There were over a thousand people in the audience and by the time the reading finished there wasn't a dry eye in the house.

I walked on stage at 7.30 p.m. on the dot, to deafening applause, and in the back of my mind I remember saying to myself: 'This'll be a good one, Sal. They are open wide.'

You see, when spirit feels openness, it comes flooding in, so the more excited and eager an audience is, the easier it will be to get those connections going.

As the applause died down, I felt her. I knew straight away she was a young girl. I could sense she was around ten or eleven years old, a pretty girl with mousy-brown hair and sad brown eyes. My heart raced, like it always does when there are children involved. I took a breath and spoke to the audience.

'I have a young girl here,' I began, as I paced the stage. In my mind I could see and feel her and I opened up my mind to let her in. I could feel her energy being pulled towards a part of the audience. She wanted her mum. My heart ached.

'She wants her mum,' I explained. 'The name is Michelle.'

Up in the circle, a lady stood. She looked in her thirties and was attractive with blonde hair and hoop earrings. She was wearing a white, open-necked clingy blouse and a black skirt. Her eyes were filled with sadness. She was shaking.

Ellie was showing me images of her life. She had been active and fun-loving.

'If I could, I would be running up and down this stage, darling,' I told her.

It usually only takes that one hint of recognition for the floodgates to open, and when Michelle heard my description she began to cry.

'My Ellie,' she said. The audience was transfixed.

The spirit, Ellie, felt her mum; the connection was made. I felt a flood of warmth wash through me towards Michelle.

'Mummy, Mummy,' I repeated as the words dropped into my head. 'I only went round the corner.'

Hearing these words, Michelle began to sob uncontrollably.

I didn't know it at the time, but Ellie was Michelle's daughter Eloise. She had died just fifteen weeks before the show and had been an animal lover and a horse rider. On the day of her death she had been excited about taking her pony to a show and had gone out to feed and groom it in the fields behind her grandparents' house where the pony was kept. As Ellie ran excitedly to her horse, her mother was a few seconds behind her, just around the corner. But in a tragic accident, just before Michelle arrived, Ellie was kicked in the head by another horse, who was excited by the food in Ellie's hand. The injury killed her.

'Where's my daddy, Andy?' I relayed. Ellie's energy was so strong I was picking up her mannerisms. I was talking like a young girl.

The man with Michelle, her husband and Ellie's father, stood up.

'That's me,' he said. He was rubbing his wife's back, supporting and comforting her, as he had done through-out the terrible weeks since their daughter's sudden death.

In my mind, Ellie took me to her house and showed me her bedroom, with the posters on the walls and photos of her on her horse. I saw her at the top of the stairs, and she was singing, her beautiful voice belting out a pop song.

'You don't hear me singing. I sing at the top of the stairs. I call you.'

Michelle nodded.

'Who's Peter?' I asked

The man with Michelle and Andy stood. He was a fam-ily friend.

An image of a cut on someone's head snapped into my mind.

'Peter, head bleeding,' I said. 'Head bleeding.'

Another woman with the group stood and explained that Peter's daughter had hurt her head.

'In my leg,' I relayed to them. 'Mummy, they put some-thing in my leg.'

Now the spirit of Ellie was showing me scenes from

after her accident. There were medical people around her, and they were putting some kind of line into her leg. I could feel her panicking. She hated needles.

'They said it would go away' – Ellie's words flowed through my mind – 'but it didn't go away.'

Weeping, Michelle nodded again. After the accident, as the medics had tried to save her life, they put injections in Ellie's leg. She hadn't liked needles, and Michelle had always been haunted by the thought of that needle phobia and how Ellie would have been scared as they tried to help her. She had told her daughter, 'It's OK. They'll be gone soon.'

By this point, I too was blinking back tears, along with the family and most of the audience. I saw a cart in a field.

'In cart is where I sit,' I explained to Michelle. 'She is saying "cart", not "car".'

'Yes, that's the horse cart,' confirmed Michelle.

Ellie was telling her mum that that was where she would be able to find the spirit of her daughter. 'If you go out there, you can feel me,' she told her mum.

'I know where she means,' nodded Michelle.

Then I saw locks of soft hair. It was shiny and clean, and I could smell fresh shampoo on it. It was a child's hair, Ellie's, mousy brown and so silky I could almost feel it running through my fingers. I clenched my fists as if to hold it. I didn't want it to slip away; I wanted to feel this beautiful girl as if she were alive again, running through the fields with her hair blowing in the breeze, her whole future ahead of her.

Then, pop! An image of hair in a freezer bag snapped into my mind.

'Her hair,' I said, 'is it in a freezer bag?' I saw an image of Michelle silently closing a bag, her eyes heavy with sadness. I mimed closing a freezer bag. 'Pop, pop, pop.'

Michelle nodded once more.

'I put it in a bag and then in a box,' she wept. 'I'm so frightened of losing her.'

Then Ellie showed me another scene. Her mum was at home, tidying up and putting shiny buttons in a box, and in the corner of the room stood Ellie, watching, full of love and longing. I knew this was a scene from after her death. Spirits are always drawn to the places they associate with love, and this is especially so for children. Ellie had returned to her home and was watching her mum, hoping with all her energy that her mum could feel her presence.

'She is watching you,' I told Michelle. 'She'll show you signs. You'll hear her.'

'I need to hear her,' she replied.

Then, in the playful way child spirit often has, little Ellie showed me a comical scene of Peter, the family friend in the audience, desperately trying to pull on a pair of shoes that were too small for him. Ellie wanted to make her parents laugh. She could see how emotional her mum was and, in that endearing way children have, she decided that the best way to make her feel better was to make her laugh.

I told Michelle what I was seeing in my mind, and the group laughed and confirmed that Peter had indeed tried to wear a pair of shoes that did not fit.

As the audience laughed at the image, I felt Ellie's own laughter tinkling in my ears.

'She thinks that's hysterical,' I said. 'Get a bigger pair of shoes, Peter!'

As if her mum and dad needed still more validation,

little Ellie gave them one more message. I saw a photo, a small passport-sized picture of Ellie, and it was grasped in her father's hand. I knew he often kissed it. It held so much energy; it held his love. This is why I ask the audience for their photos and mementoes; photographs are powerful tools for mediums. They hold the love and the energy. Spirits focus on such objects.

'Daddy has a photo,' I said, repeating Ellie's words. 'He kisses my photo.' By now, I was crying freely. Andy let go of his wife and raised the palm of his hand for the theatre to see. Clutched inside was a small photo. Ellie, the girl whose spirit had amazed everyone, looked out from that picture.

Tiny Miracles

Parents like Ellie's are so brave, and when they get messages I hope the audience realizes just how courageous they are to come to a psychic show and try to connect with their little lost children. Each night, when the odd and the strange and, frankly, sometimes the comical is happening on stage, it can be easy for the people watching it all unfold to lose sight of just how incredible the events going on are.

It's a big deal getting a message from a dead person, believe me. I never take it for granted. Each one of those messages, no matter how seemingly bizarre or trivial, is a little miracle. That is why I always implore people to take the messages I give, even if they appear tenuous at first. We get so many people after a show who say, 'Oh yes, that message was for me, but I was too embarrassed to stand up,' and it is such a pity. It takes so much energy for spirit to come through and make contact – we should welcome them in and grasp whatever it is they have to offer with both hands. They are presenting us with gifts.

Ellie's mum said after the reading that she will now sit at the top of the stairs where Ellie's spirit returns to sing and sing her daughter's favourite songs and feel her daughter singing along with her. It's humbling to know that the reason she can do this with hope and faith is because she decided to buy a ticket to come to one of my shows. The reading probably only amounted to five minutes, but in those five minutes maybe her life changed for ever. Maybe she saw the silver lining on the cloud that had darkened her life. I certainly hope so, with all my heart.

Then again, as is often the case with powerful readings, I doubt that Michelle buying that ticket was completely random: I reckon Ellie might have had something to do with it. Because they orchestrate things, spirits do. They influence what we do, and I know for a fact that they influence who comes to the shows, and even where they sit. Sometimes they even join together to make sure their plans work.

I know, I know! It sounds far-fetched, but how do you explain what happened to me in a theatre in the Midlands when the energy of two babies came through one night?

'One is a little boy called Ben . . . Benjy,' I explained. I could see him at the edge of my subconscious perception: he was tiny, much smaller than a normal baby, his skin paper-thin, almost see-through. He looked somehow alien, and his big, dark eyes were staring intently and blinking.

'He's absolutely gorgeous,' I told the audience. But there was something wrong with his head. Then he spoke to me.

Now, I know babies can't talk in life, but in death everything is different. In death the physical rules that restrain us no longer exist. Babies, even babies that are stillborn, can communicate, because we are all born with a soul and the energy that makes up that soul transcends language. The words I hear and feel when I'm communicating with the dead are not made of sounds that you and I would recognize as speech; they are thought patterns, and my brain interprets them. It's as if I'm translating from a foreign language into English.

So Ben's energy, his thought process, resonated with mine, and I heard his words.

'My head wasn't the right shape,' I said to the audience, casting my gaze along the rows of faces to see if the message made sense to anyone.

A woman in the audience dressed in black stood to take the message. I felt a connection instantly as the baby in spirit joined with his mother. She was a pretty woman, in her twenties.

'A little boy? With a slightly misshapen head?' I asked.

She nodded a confirmation.

'His skull hadn't formed properly.' She began to cry. During pregnancy, she had suffered a terrible bleed, and a scan had revealed that her child was suffering a genetic condition that meant his head was not growing as it should. The chances were remote that he would survive, and she had to make the agonizing decision to induce early to see if the doctors could save him. He survived just a few hours before he passed away.

Another name came through.

'Who's Maria? She's next to you?'

A lady in pink sitting in the seat next to the bereaved mother raised her hand. 'I'm Maria,' she said.

'Are you two together?' I asked.

They didn't know each other and had only met that night when they sat down together.

Confused, I assumed it was a classic case of one spirit hijacking the reading of another when it spotted a loved one nearby, a case of a spirit's energy being drawn to the strong connection of another.

Then the lady in pink said something amazing.

'We've just met tonight, but I've lost two babies.'

I was gobsmacked. That was why these two ladies had come tonight. Both of them happened to be sitting next to the other, both with babies in spirit. It was no coincidence, no way.

'There are two babies here,' I told them. 'They've come because they knew you two would be together.' The lady in pink explained that she had prayed all day that they would make an appearance. And even more incredibly, one of her babies had died of exactly the same condition that the first lady's baby had suffered from.

Both of them were in tears.

'Both comfort one another,' I told them. 'You are friends for life.' I could feel the satisfaction flowing from spirit as the babies showed me more. I felt the presence of another little girl. The woman in pink, Maria, confirmed that she had also lost a girl.

'They are with other relatives,' I told them. I explained that one baby was with a grandfather and the other was with two women relatives. 'They are not alone,' I explained. 'They are in Heaven surrounded by love and their souls are being taken care of. They are your children. Because they didn't live long enough for you doesn't mean they didn't exist.'

The audience applauded.

After the show, I had time to reflect on what an amazing message I had been privileged to channel that night. There were forces at play bringing those two women together that were more mysterious and powerful than we'll ever understand. It was an energy of pure love, and it proved that even the psychic energy created by the spirit of a baby can be a real force for good. That night those little babies were putting their mums in touch to help heal them.

Paradise Awaits

Bereaved parents come to me and to my shows because they have burning questions which they need answered. They need to know if their children are at peace, if they are with someone, if they suffered, if they could have done anything differently to keep their children alive. And, most of all, they want answers to the one question that burns at their soul and makes it impossible for them to move on. They want to know why.

I don't profess to have all the answers, but I hope even in only a small way I help the parents who come to see me.

It doesn't matter what the setting is, whether it's a one-on-one reading or in a theatre, when I'm talking to a person and linking them to spirit world I'm focused entirely on them; I'm oblivious to everyone else. Once that link is established, it's as if we are tied together in time and space.

The one comfort I can offer all bereaved parents is that their children would not have passed alone, no matter what the circumstances were on earth plane. There would have been someone in spirit waiting to care and nurture the soul of the departed. There always is. Death is not a lonely place, not for anyone. And whatever pain the child may have felt when it was alive, it is dissolved away on death, replaced by bliss and peace and love.

As for the biggie, as for the 'Why?', all I can say is what I have said before and what I truly believe, having had a lifetime of psychic experience: none of us goes before we are meant to go, which is especially hard to understand when it comes to the death of a child.

It's human nature to think that there is something we could have done, that they should have lived for longer, that their death was a massive injustice. But people are like roses. We bloom and we are beautiful. Some of us bloom all summer long but others bloom just for a few days before they fade and die. It is all part of the grand design. It doesn't make bereavement any easier, but that's the way it is. Those, I'm afraid, are the rules.

When a mum comes to me with those burning questions, full of confusion and grief, all I can offer is the truth as I receive it.

One mum I'll always remember came to me after her unborn daughter was snatched from her in a tragic car accident. She was thirty-four weeks pregnant and looking forward to life with her new child. But after the crash, by the time her daughter was born, she had stopped breathing. This daughter came to me straight away and showed me another baby, and gave me the name Christie. The mother explained that her friend was called Christie and that she had recently given birth.

'Your daughter has been around the baby,' I told her. I saw an image of her baby, a beautiful little soul who had been born with a hair lip. I explained this, and the mother explained that her baby girl had been born perfect except for this little mark on her top lip. She immediately knew I had her little baby girl with me in spirit.

'You are going to know she is with you,' I reassured her.

There are people who say that to give messages from children is morbid but, no, this amazing ability I have gives the mothers I meet comfort. I know it does. And what could be a better gift than that?

A Close Shave with a Man with a Gun

You wouldn't think it, but us psychics meet some pretty unscrupulous characters sometimes. We don't all sit at home in the comfort of our living rooms staring into crystal balls for little old ladies who want to contact their pets in spirit. Sometimes, as a medium, you get what I like to call a 'wrong 'un' knocking on your door. Let's call them morally ambiguous, shall we? Knaves and thieves, scallywags and scoundrels – you know the type. I've had plenty come through my door. I don't know why they radiate towards me, but I suspect it's to do with my family history.

Back in Fulham when I was growing up, my family was well known. They were the kind of local 'faces' all working-class communities used to have, and probably still do to some extent. They weren't gangsters in the traditional sense, they weren't Mafia; they didn't run a crime empire, but they did have influence and you wouldn't want to cross them. They would have words with people for you if you were in trouble, they could make certain problems go away and they were feared and respected in equal measure. They were tough but just, and they didn't victimize innocent people. Back in those days, there was still some concept of honour. The 'faces' in my family could be harsh if you got on the wrong side of them but they were always fair in their dealings. They weren't out-and-out crooks, but let's just say, sometimes, what they did fell into a bit of a grey area where the law was concerned.

I believe that because of this part of my history, certain members of society are drawn to me for readings. More often than not they come later in life – older crooks. I suspect they come when their consciences are troubling them, when they've reached an age when the exuberance of youth is long gone and they've started to consider the implications of their past actions and what the effects will be of some of the bad things they've done in their younger lives. They've mellowed. Maybe they're looking for some kind of absolution. If they are, though, they're looking in the wrong place. I'm not a priest, I don't take confessions and I don't have any power that would allow me to forgive sins. As far as I'm concerned, that power resides only with one being, the higher being that watches over us all.

Other times, I think maybe these sorts of clients come to test out the theory that there is an afterlife. They come along to see if I can give them concrete proof of a Heaven and a Hell. They want to know if they will be punished for their misdeeds when they die. Then, I suppose, if they're convinced, they'll go home, hedge their bets and start atoning for past sins.

For the record, I don't hold much truck with the traditional theory of Hell. I don't believe in an underworld presided over by a horned Satan where all the bad souls are cast to burn for all eternity. No, I think Hell is more subtle and clever than that.

I believe Hell is here, on earth. I know that sounds very negative and that there are many beautiful things on earth and much happiness to be had in life, but I believe that because the afterlife – Heaven or divinity – is such a wondrous, amazing place, the souls of those who have done really bad things in their lives (the Osama bin Ladens, the Harold Shipmans and the Myra Hindleys of this world) get sent back here. The gates of Heaven are shut in their faces and their souls are cast back to earth, not as evil spirits, but to live again in new bodies, to purge the evil. I don't mean to be glib, but I think they are put through the wash again to see if they come out whiter. And I think this process probably continues until all the stains of evil are washed away, and then they are allowed into Heaven. I've definitely had a few clients who probably would not qualify for the afterlife the first time round and may well be sent back through the psychic washing machine for another cycle!

But despite what they have done in their past, I sometimes feel strangely drawn to people on the fringes of society like this. Not because I condone law-breaking, not at all, but because in a way, I find them strangely fascinating. I like to know what makes them tick, what goes on inside their minds. I've always been fascinated with the dark side of human nature and the psychological impulses that make us choose wrong from right. I want to know what drives them.

One of these morally ambiguous clients ended up becoming a good friend of mine. For all kinds of legal reasons, I'll not name her. As far as I know, she's on the run now and she's never been brought to justice. Let's call her Sophia. She was a member of the aristocracy, her family having links to royalty in Europe, and she herself was originally from the Continent. She married into what she thought was money. Her husband had a title and he was hypnotized by her – she was stunning. She was a tall, leggy blonde with striking features. Her skin was flawless porcelain and she had that air about her that some aristocrats exude. I suppose it's all in the breeding. She didn't go out of her way to appear aloof, but somehow she seemed a notch above everyone else. She was also an intelligent, cultured woman with a bit of a wild side. She loved art and architecture and she lived with her entrepreneur husband in a beautiful house in one of the poshest areas of London. Their listed-building home was full of antiques and works of art. She especially loved antique books – expensive first editions – and had a library full of leather-bound tomes.

She came to me after another well-heeled friend recommended me. Initially, she came to see me for one of the usual reasons: she had doubts about her relationship. She would book up regular readings and, as the months went on, she began to cross over the client divide I try to maintain. Rather than sticking to her allotted appointment times, she would ring out of hours and over the weekend. She began to eat into my personal space. John must have been a better judge of character than me at the time, because he was quite cold with her. He could see what she was doing, that she was encroaching on my life, and I knew it too, but I liked her so I didn't care. Despite her failings, and she had many, she was entertaining company.

Even when the money she paid me for the readings started to dry up and the cheques started bouncing, there would always be an excuse, and she would smooth any problems over by buying me an expensive dinner at some classy London restaurant.

In those days, it would take a lot for me to refuse to see a client. Maybe I was naive back then, but I can only remember one lady I refused to continue seeing. She was a horrid person, a woman who had married into money, but she was mean with it and mean to everyone around her. She let her newfound wealth corrupt her, and I drew the line when I was reading for her one day and was shown the image of passports locked in a safe. I knew they belonged to the people who worked on the estate her husband owned – the people she viewed as her servants. Most of them, I assumed, were illegal immigrants, and she kept their passports under lock and key to keep them in bondage to her. I had seen the way she behaved towards her stuff and I was disgusted with what she was doing to those poor people. So when I picked up the passports in the reading, I told her I knew what she was doing with them and that I didn't want her custom any longer. She was incensed that I would have the nerve to refuse her money and we didn't part on cordial terms.

However, that wasn't the first time I had let someone nasty know that I was privy to incriminating information about them. Many years ago, a gentleman came to see me and, as soon as he shook my hand, I knew he was a wife-beater. I saw an image of him standing over his cowering wife, his hand raised and his teeth gritted in a snarl.

'You can stop hitting her for a start,' I said as he sat down.

His face drained, and he sat fidgeting and denying any knowledge of what I'd told him. I knew, though, and I hope that I gave him enough of a shock that, after that day, he stopped what he was doing.

Sophia was different though. She was generous of spirit

and would have been generous with her wealth too, had she had any. She enjoyed the benefit of credit, which has always been dished out to those who appear wealthy, just as readily as it was to the general public before the most recent credit crunch. Using their aristocratic credentials, she and her husband found it easy to persuade people to extend them lines of credit. They borrowed money and they borrowed goods. They would even persuade antique dealers to lend them items for their homes. But they could not stave off the effects of several ill-advised business ventures and, inevitably, their lifestyle caught up with them. As the creditors closed in, they did what any self-respecting cad would do: they did a moonlight flit and skipped the country, owing I don't know how much. I didn't know this at the time of course. As far as I could tell, they had just moved and not told me.

I thought that would be the last I ever heard of them. However, several months later, when the dust had settled, I received a call.

'Darling Sally, how are you? Sorry I didn't say goodbye, but a few things came up and we had to leave the country with some urgency.' The syrupy, heavily accented voice was Sophia's. I should have been mad with her, I should have hung up the phone – after all, she owed me money – but by then our relationship had turned into friendship, and she was one of those people you just couldn't stay mad with for too long. I was actually pleased to hear from her.

She explained that after a 'spot of unforeseen trouble', as she described it, she and her husband were now living in a mansion overlooking the ocean in South Africa.

'You must come out. I insist,' she told me.

I silenced the alarm bells ringing in the back of my head and agreed. What can I say? I'm a sucker for a bit of adventure.

And so, about six months after Sophia had disappeared off the radar in the UK, I was met by her at Cape Town airport and chauffeured to the most amazing mansion in the hills just outside the city. The house had the best of everything. Every room was full of amazing antiques, the pool terrace had views that went on for miles, and the property was staffed by attentive servants.

It seemed that Sophia had really landed on her feet – which was why I was so surprised that she was so jumpy. She should have been in her element, but instead she was preoccupied and vaguely paranoid about going out of the walled compound the property was in.

One day, her husband asked me to accompany him to have a look at another property they were thinking of renting nearer the coast. This one was even bigger than the one they currently lived in.

'The views of the ocean are better,' he explained.

Sophia decided to stay at home, so I went with him on my own. We drove along isolated roads, and he looked decidedly nervous throughout the journey. I noticed that he was sweating profusely for much of the two hours we were together and, whenever there was a vehicle behind, he would look anxiously in the rear-view mirror and speed up.

The house was amazing, and in a beautiful part of the region.

It was only a few days later, in a late-night conversation fuelled by vintage wine, that Sophia opened up to me.

They had got themselves involved in some business

deals with some very shady characters and Sophia had heard that their lives were at risk. There were people looking for them, and there was a bounty on their heads: they were wanted dead or alive.

Then she revealed that, on the trip I had taken with her husband, we were indeed followed . . . by a hitman! Seeing me, he had decided not to act. He didn't want to complicate matters by involving an innocent bystander. I had been a human shield – little old me, Sally the psychic. The people who were after Sophia and her husband had let them know how close they had come to exacting their revenge. To say I was shaken was an understatement. I went mad. I couldn't believe my life had been put at such a risk and soon afterwards I left South Africa. I have never been so glad to get home.

John, in his usual understated way, sighed when I told him. 'I told you they were trouble,' he tutted.

I heard from Sophia a few times again after that trip, but gradually the phone calls stopped. I never got the money I was owed and, with the benefit of a few years' hindsight, I look back on the episode with some fondness and try to laugh about it. I'd actually saved a life that day – unintentionally, of course.

The last I heard, Sophia and her husband had done another flit. I have no idea where they are now, but when they left their home they must have been in a hurry, because they left everything behind, even her designer handbags. Their car was found abandoned at the airport. According to the reports I read, none of the antiques they had furnished the mansion with had ever belonged to them: they'd all been scammed from unsuspecting antique dealers.

We Forget Our Pain

I honestly do not know what will await Sophia and her husband in the afterlife. They were not evil, and the harm they inflicted was financial rather than physical – not that that is any excuse for illegal behaviour. I think perhaps they'll be given the opportunity to come back again and put right their wrongs in another life. For all I know, they could be dead now. I hope not. If the reports of their crimes are correct, they deserve to be punished just the same as everyone else, but Sophia had a good heart underneath it all. She just got sucked into a lifestyle she couldn't afford. I guess when you have a title people expect you to be a certain way; they expect you to be rich and successful, even if you're not.

While the afterlife of the perpetrators of crime is an uncertain path, for the victims it is more certain.

In my work, I've connected with many spirits of victims. I have read for victims' families, and each time it breaks my heart. In the case of murder, a life snuffed out is such a huge waste, and so difficult to overcome for the loved ones left behind. Then of course there are the families who cannot get closure, the families whose loved ones have gone missing and are desperate for some clue as to what has happened. These are always such hard readings to do, because sometimes I have to tell mothers, fathers and relatives information they do not want to hear. But once again, when spirit world gives me details of a violent and unpleasant death, of pain and suffering, it's my duty to pass these details on, because the fact that spirit is giving the details to me means that those details are important. All I can do is pass them on in a sympathetic way, and I do. I feel the pain and misery crime and murder cause every time it intrudes on my psychic mind.

The one thing all family and friends of people who have been killed by criminals want to know is whether their loved ones are at peace. These deaths are always so violent and unexpected they leave a terrible stain on the conscious minds of the ones left behind. It's easy to become haunted by thoughts of a person's last minutes when their life has been so cruelly snatched away that after a while that's all you see: the pain and the suffering and the violence. And this in turn makes it impossible to move on. Victims of crime who have died horrifically at the hands of others are in danger of becoming defined by their deaths and not by their lives, and that is a tragedy as, on earth plane, what matters most is how we lived and what we did and how much love we had in our lives, not what happened at the end. That is a tiny splinter of the story and one not worth dwelling on. You could have a lifetime of love and happiness but be murdered by a serial killer and the killing is what everyone remembers. It's unfair, as if the killer doesn't just take a life but the memories of that life as well.

That's why we must remember good people for who they were and not for what happened to them. If a relative, spouse or friend has had a dreadful passing, it's important to remember that death is only the beginning – the beginning of the journey for our soul. Our existence goes through different phases, and death is just another transition, like when a grub changes into a beautiful butterfly. Death is the blinking of an eye, and what happens in that split second is irrelevant to what came before and what comes after.

Only the body suffers. The pain we feel is confined to the physical part of our being – our vessel, our flesh and blood. Once we die, this is cast off, it is just our remains; our soul is free from it and any suffering it endured.

However we die, whether peacefully at home aged 110 lying on soft, clean Egyptian-cotton sheets with our head on a lovely plump duck-down pillow with all our loved ones around us, or whether we are murdered in an atrocious way, we go to the same place. And here we are free from everything except the love we had on earth. All the pain and suffering, all the confusion and fear we might have felt on passing is taken away. It becomes utterly meaningless because where we end up after death is so beautiful. It's like going on the holiday of a lifetime. You may have had delays at the airport, and you may have had a terrible flight, but as soon as you lie on that beach with the sound of the waves lapping at the shore and the warm sun kissing your skin, you forget all that.

Often, when murder victims come through to me, they show me the scenes of their deaths, the confusion and pain, the brutality and their fear, and they might say things that make it seem as if they are angry at what happened, but they are just mirroring our anger because they are connected to us. They're showing us their passing so we recognize who they are. Heaven isn't an angry place. Victims come through with images of their violent ends so we can recognize them and, once that connection is made, they only have messages of love.

Such a Waste

I love doing shows in the home counties – for one thing, it means I get a relatively early night! So I was in good spirits when we pulled up to the Central Theatre in Chatham, Kent, for a show in 2009. The drive had been short and I was rested and relaxed, ready for whatever spirit deemed to throw at me that night.

After the usual preparations, I stepped out to deafening applause and said a big 'hello' to the audience. I always start the evening with a trademark 'psychic wave', where the audience all wave in unison. It looks funny so it's a good ice-breaker, and it also helps raise the energy levels in the room. Everyone laughing and doing something together has the effect of harmonizing the energy in the auditorium. Don't ask me how, it just seems to work, and if it helps with the messages, who am I to argue?

He was one of the first spirits to come through, and his energy was strong and purposeful. He was polite, and I could tell straight away he was a teenager. The energy of a spirit *feels* different from spirit to spirit and I can tell which belongs to a child, which to a teenager, which to an adult and which to a senior citizen. This was definitely a very young man. And along with it I felt that twinge of sadness I always get when I realize it must have been a life snatched short.

I saw him in my mind's eye. He was around eighteen

years old, stocky, and had short curly brown hair and expressive blue eyes. He was whispering to me and, as I focused my mind into the thought patterns that were playing through it, I picked up the words 'Rob' and 'hill'.

'I have a young man here,' I told the audience. 'He says, "You can call me Rob," and I am getting the word "hill". Does that mean anything to anyone?'

I looked up out into the auditorium and, in the middle of the audience, a hand went up. The lady it belonged to took the microphone from one of my helpers and stood up with two other young women. They all looked similar, all dressed for a night out, and they radiated a very positive, fun energy. There was an older lady – the one who had raised her hand – and two younger ones who I presumed were her daughters.

'You look like the Nolans,' I laughed.

The young man in spirit recognized them; I felt that familiar warm glow as the energy between them joined. Then the images started. I felt slightly wobbly as I was shown chaotic scenes. I saw blood on a pavement, I heard shouting and crying, I saw a face screwed into a violent grimace and I felt a feeling of fear, adrenaline and terrified confusion.

'This one is going to make me sad,' I explained, and tears sprang to my eyes. I knew I had the spirit of a murder victim with me. I asked the women who this Rob who had come through to me was.

They explained that he was a childhood friend of theirs, and he had been killed in a fight the previous year.

'What's the relevance of the word "hill"?' I asked.

'That's our surname,' the women answered.

The audience gasped.

I was now being the shown the last moments of Rob's life. The scene was a bar. Rob was trying to protect someone.

'He put up a fight,' I said as the images and feelings flashed into my mind. I felt a surge of pain going through my body – hot, like a knife.

'I feel it on the right-hand side,' I explained. 'Someone got hold of him from behind. I can see it as if it was happening in front of me.'

The older woman of the three explained that Rob was an actor who had been stabbed and killed on a night out. I later learned that his full name was Robert Knox. He had overcome the adversity of being bullied as a young teenager to begin a career in films and, until May 2008, it seemed he had a glittering future ahead of him. At the age of twelve he was subjected to a three-year campaign of bullying over his weight, finally forcing his parents to move him to a new school. But rather than let this episode ruin his life, Rob chose to draw strength from it and to follow his acting dreams. He had been acting since the age of eleven and had appeared in the 2004 film *King Arthur*, the BBC comedy *After You've Gone*, *The Bill* and *Tonight with Trevor McDonald*, as well as the Channel 4 reality show *Trust Me, I'm a Teenager*. But his big break came when he won a part in the hugely popular Harry Potter films. He played the Hogwarts student Marcus Belby in *Harry Potter and the Half-Blood Prince* and was signed to appear in *Harry Potter and the Deathly Hallows*. Rob had a wonderful life stretching before him. However, just a few weeks after completing filming for the movie Rob was out in a bar in Sidcup, Kent, when a man started a fight with his brother. Rob tried to defend him, but the man was a knife-carrying maniac and he stabbed Rob and several other people. Rob died on the pavement outside the bar.

Now his childhood friends had come to my show, and Rob was there with them.

'Tell him we love him,' the older woman said, blinking back tears.

In my mind another name came to me.

'Who is Zoe? Is that his mum?' I asked.

'No, I'm Zoe,' she answered.

Then he whispered something in my head and started to giggle.

'Amy, where is my ball?' he said.

It was another one of those occasions where the message doesn't seem to fit the tone of the reading. I had been shown a scene of devastation and a talented young life cut down on the cusp of a bright future, but now there was a mischievous voice whispering about a ball. As ever, I put my faith in spirit and repeated to the women what I was picking up.

One of the girls – she must have been in her late teens or early twenties – drew a sharp breath in. She was dressed in a beige jacket with a rose-print T-shirt on underneath. Her hair was cut into a shiny auburn bob.

'He's saying, "Amy, what have you done with my ball? Where is it?"' I said.

'I'm Amy,' she told me. 'Rob and I used to play together when we were little. He used to come to my house and we'd play in the garden with a ball. I still have it at home somewhere.'

Then Rob's attention must have turned to something

else. An image of a backpack slotted into my head like a slide into a projector, and he was showing me a young man, someone travelling or leaving home.

I asked the women what this meant, and they explained that Rob's brother had just got a contract to go and work in Spain and that he would soon be leaving the country.

It was an amazing reading. I didn't know the full details of the case or of Rob's passing until after the show, when someone in my office explained who he was. That he appeared to the audience that night to connect with his friends and gently have a laugh with them shows that even the worst wounds, physical or emotional, do not linger after death.

Hell on Earth

It's always an initial shock to connect with the spirit of a murder victim – not because they mean to or want to shock but because of the intensity of the information they give. You have to have a strong stomach and the ability to look beyond the message to the spirit delivering it. And, sometimes, although the spirits don't mean any trouble, there are repercussions from what I see and pass on.

At a show in Northern Ireland, I once caused such a stir there was a radio-show phone-in about me the following day. I can't recall the exact details of the reading – the names and the locations – but I still shiver when I think about what I was shown.

I was given the image of a young man. He had been sound asleep in his bed when suddenly he was awoken by the sound of people crashing through the door. The wood on the frame splintered as three men, their faces covered with balaclavas, stormed into his room. Before he had time to react, he was roughly grabbed, punched and kicked then shot in the head. It was over in seconds. His bloody body was rolled up in his duvet and taken to isolated woods, where he was buried.

Because of the political sensitivities in Northern Ireland, and because of the strong religious beliefs held by parts of the community there, my reading was not welcome, and the following day there was a debate on the local radio station in which I was the main topic of conversation. What made it worse was that I had a two-night booking, and so, after a hostile reaction from elements of the community, I had to go back to the theatre in the middle of the media storm. Luckily, the audience was friendly.

Another time, a murder victim came through at a show and gave me the name Colin. I explained to the audience that I was seeing the aftermath of a brutal fight in a home and a blood-stained runner in the hallway. The imagery was spot on and the victim's parents, whose surname was Collins, were in the audience. But, tragically, I felt a family connection with the crime.

'Did you kill your son?' I said to the father.

'No,' he replied. 'It was my other son.'

A family row had descended into horror when one brother stabbed the other in the kitchen. The victim had staggered down the hallway and bled to death on the rug. What a senseless waste of life.

Staring through a window into the dying moments of a person's life can be harrowing when that life ends in violence. The ones that really affect me and chill me to the bone are the sadistic murders when the victim is a defence-less woman. Perhaps it's because I'm a woman and have young daughters, but those sorts of murders, the really sick ones perpetrated by men who get a kick out of controlling women, always leave their mark on me. Sometimes it's hard to wash those marks off: they remain etched in my mind, like scar tissue.

I'll never fail to be horrified by the awful and cruel ways people will find to end each others' lives. Like I mentioned earlier, sometimes Hell is right here on earth. Sometimes what people do to each other and the pain they inflict is beyond comprehension.

Thankfully, crimes like this are rare, but I came across one in Manchester that left an indelible mark on me.

The auditorium was full. The show was at the Palace Theatre, an imposing building with an air of grandeur about it. Nothing marked the day out as any different. John had driven to the venue and, as usual, we had bickered on the way about directions and then about parking when he arrived in the city. Before the show I was nervous, and I don't always get nervous. Often I get excited, but rarely nervous. When I do, however, the show that follows is usually a humdinger. Don't ask me why; that just seems to be the way it happens. Perhaps it's something about the energy I'm giving off; perhaps spirit senses my anxiety and makes an extra effort to help me out.

I'd only been on stage a few minutes when I felt her. She was giving off the unmistakable energy of distress. Through me she was channelling a replay of her last minutes on earth, and they were not pleasant.

Hold on, Sally, I told myself. This is going to be a tough one.

Sometimes, when I feel snatches of information and I know the details are going to be gruesome, I almost resist. It's as if I have a defence mechanism that tries to protect me. But every message is important, and I have to remain open, so that night I opened myself and let the spirit in. She was a young girl and, as I felt her, I raised my hands to the audience and crossed my palms.

'My hands are tied,' I told them. 'They are bound up.'

And then the air was forced out of my chest. I felt a

huge weight push down, winding me and knocking the breath from my lungs.

'I feel as if my chest is pushed in, like someone has just sat on my chest.'

And then I felt light, as if I was drifting away, untethered.

'I have gone,' I told the audience.

Whoever this girl was, she had just hit me with such a disconcerting bolt of psychic energy it left me shaken and disorientated.

A woman in the crowd stood to take the message. She wore a grey top with the words 'Kiss and tell' printed on it and her red hair was pulled back from her face.

'That's my cousin Stephanie,' she said. 'She was only twenty-one and her boyfriend murdered her in her bed. He tied her up.'

The images Stephanie was showing me became even more vivid. One after the other, I felt huge weights being slammed on my chest. SLAM! SLAM! And I saw paving stones – great, heavy concrete paving slabs.

'Oh my God,' I said. 'He put garden slabs on her chest.' I was shaking and gasping for breath.

The woman confirmed what I was being shown. 'He went out and he got a slab and he threw it on her. The police said it was the second one that killed her.'

More disturbing images came flooding in. I saw the killer, his weasel face twisted into a grimace and his stained teeth biting down on the victim's toes.

'Oh my life. He bit the toes on her right foot – why did he do that?'

The woman answered that he had lost his temper because

Stephanie wanted to go out and celebrate her birthday with her friends and had asked her boyfriend to babysit for her.

In my mind I was in the room where the attack took place. The vividness of it terrified me. I was crying openly.

'I can't bear this,' I sobbed. 'He did things to her before. He used to pinch her. This is dreadful. I've never had anything like this before. I can see his teethmarks in her feet.'

And then, as the scenes playing out in my mind reached a sickening crescendo, there was calm. As quickly as it started, the maelstrom of violence ended and was replaced by serenity and peace. Stephanie was showing me how quickly dying itself recedes and how peaceful the afterlife is. She was showing me that she no longer suffers.

Shakily, I smiled. I understood. She didn't want to upset me or her family. She had to show me the horrible stuff so I would appreciate what a good place she was now in.

'She's come here to tell you she isn't in pain any more,' I told her family.

The Horror Takes Its Toll

I have no idea what the long-term effects of what I do will be. I like to think it will energize me and I'll be toddling around on stage when I'm ninety, talking to the dead and still selling out theatres. Maybe the psychic energy is something like formaldehyde and I'll be preserved in it, like a psychic pickled egg!

Hopefully, it won't work in reverse. Hopefully, the effort of plugging into the psychic mains each night is not sucking the energy away from me. Hopefully, it's not like radiation and won't build up and up until it makes me ill.

Like I say, I haven't a clue what the long-term effects will be on my body. I know that, each night after a show, I feel completely energized and full of beans, and I'm hoping this is a positive sign. However, on rare occasions, the messages I get are so difficult, so vivid and graphic, they wear me out. On even rarer occasions they have made me physically sick. The mental effort of channelling two murder victims, each of whom had died a horrible death, actually made me collapse.

The show was in Hampshire, it was a midweek spring evening, and the messages had been pouring in. Then the girl arrived.

She came through nervously, showing herself to me in human form, willowy and pale. She wore nightclothes and looked no more than twenty-one years old. In my mind I was transported to a location.

It's a strange feeling being moved through the energy of spirit. It can be disorientating. You have to keep a close focus on what is spirit and what is earth plane. The scene materializes in my mind. The best way I can describe it is it being like an old-fashioned television being turned on. In the days before flatscreen and LCD, TVs had cathode rays in them that needed to warm up and, as they did, the picture slowly came into focus. That's just how it looks in my mind when I'm shown a scene. My body and the conscious part of my mind remains where it is (it would look weird if I floated off too!) but the part of my mind that connects to spirit goes on a walkabout. The Sally rooted in the physical realm commentates on what the Sally in the psychic realm is seeing.

On this particular night, the girl had appeared and I was taken to a copse. It was night there, and dark. There was a hum of traffic nearby, and the outer edges of the copse were lit by orange streetlights and the dim glow from nearby windows. It was a small patch of woodland in a built-up area, isolated and abandoned. There were broken bottles and bits of rubbish strewn on the ground. It looked like the kind of place where drunks and junkies congregate after dark, the kind of place most people would rather steer clear of. I knew as soon as the girl came through that she had been murdered. She didn't have to show me: it was there in her energy, like a hallmark.

I described the scene to the audience and explained that the spirit I had connected to had been murdered. A pretty young girl raised her hand.

'Someone took this girl's life?' I asked her.

'Yes,' she confirmed in a soft voice. 'It happened over eleven years ago.'

As is so often the case, once the connection was made, the images became more defined.

I saw the murderer, his evil face leering in my mind. I saw what he did to the girl and, although here is not the place to go into detail, it was disturbing and harrowing.

'A very, very, very sick person,' I told the girl. Then, seeing what he did to his victim, I worried out loud: 'Do they have him?'

Thankfully, he had been caught, tried and imprisoned. The murderer was the victim's boyfriend, and he had been given life. Despite confirmation from the girl in the audience, I still felt a sense of unease, as if there was a loose end that needed tying up.

'There was a light in the distance, like a star, but it's a light from a bedroom window, or maybe it's flats because I'm far away. It could be a tall building,' I explained.

The girl told me that the murder had happened in the victim's bedroom. I was confused.

'Why am in a copse? Why am I in a wooded area?'

There appeared to be no connection between this murder and the place I'd been shown. It was such a distinctive death I knew there couldn't be two of them, so why the location? What was the relevance of it?

Once again, however, there was no mistake, and spirit moved in to amaze me and reveal what was happening. Just a few seats along from the lady I had been speaking to, another woman stood. This is where it gets really spooky, because that lady knew the first lady. They hadn't come together but they happened to be sitting in the same row a few seats apart. And the second lady also had a murdered friend in spirit. Her body was discovered in a copse. In my mind, I was seeing the location of one girl's murder from the scene of the other's. And both victims had known each other; they went to school together.

Suddenly, I felt a burning sensation in my ear. Spirit doesn't mean to hurt but this was uncomfortable enough to make me raise my hand to the side of my head. I relayed the details, and the woman in the audience explained that the killer had torn an earring from his victim's ear.

'He wanted a souvenir,' I said with a shiver. Then a warning echoed in my head.

'He had done dreadful things to four other women,' I relayed. 'Have they got him?'

The woman confirmed my worst fears. She shook her head. The man who had done these terrible things was still at large: a serial killer.

I returned to the first lady. I was being shown videos and books and photographs scattered around. I saw the killer in the doorway, but my view of him was restricted, as if I was looking through a letterbox. I could feel my heart racing: I was being shown the victim's last moments on earth.

The lady in the audience confirmed that the killer had taken photos of his victim after he killed her and that she was found wrapped in a duvet, which she would have hidden under as he came for her, affording her a restricted view of her attacker.

Despite the sickening imagery, I could still sense the peace and calm of spirit. The victim wanted people to know she was at peace; she wanted the woman in the audience to be the messenger, to let her loved ones know she was in Heaven.

As the spirits left and others came in, I felt drained and unsteady on my feet. Even the knowledge that the victims were no longer suffering failed to lift the fog and, as the evening wore on, I became increasingly weary. It took a huge effort to get through the show, and as soon as I came off stage I was violently ill. I was soaked in cold sweat, shaking and vomiting. For the first time ever I was unable to go to the front of house and meet the fans after the show. It's one of the parts of my appearances that I love, the opportunity to meet the audience, and I do it religiously. But this night I was washed out and ill and could hardly walk. I felt terrible for letting people down but, literally, there was nothing I could do. I couldn't even speak for fifteen minutes. I'd never felt like that before. To this day, I believe it was because of the content and intensity of the readings. Looking back now, I'm amazed that the two women happened to be sitting so close to each other, and both happened to know separate murder victims who both appeared that night. The energy it took to orchestrate that must have been unreal.

Several months later, I was struck down again after giving a powerful reading that no one in the auditorium took. The spirit was another murder victim, and she had been shot in the head, rolled in a carpet and buried under a shed. As I recounted these terrible events, the victim showed me her burial and I could feel earth filling my mouth and suffocating me. My legs started to buckle and I was bathed one again in a cold sweat. It was a horrible, unnerving feeling and one I don't think I'll ever get used to.

Usually with the really dark stuff I can switch it off like a DVD, I can protect myself from it. But sometimes, in order to let spirits say what they want to say, I have to open myself up and hope for the best.

Give a Ghost a Chance

'My house is haunted,' the woman on the other end of the phone explained. She was breathless and worried. 'They make noises,' she said. 'They rattle the pipes and shut doors. They turn the lights on at night.'

'So what's the problem?' I asked.

'Well . . . they're ghosts. I want them gone. They're freaking me out. I want an exorcism.' I stifled a laugh.

'Like in the movie?' I asked.

'Yes, I want whatever it is sent back to Hell, or wherever it came from in the first place.'

'What exactly are they doing that scares you so much?'

She sighed, and spoke very slowly and purposefully to me. 'They. Are. Haunting. My. House.'

Now, I can understand that people feel a little unsettled when it comes to what we describe as paranormal activity. By its very nature it is supernatural; it's not what we expect in the world we live in. Ghosts, apparitions, spirits – they all belong in another world, and when they find their way through to ours it can make the hairs on the back of your neck stand up. But is spiritual activity scary? In the movies perhaps. But in my experience there has only ever been a handful of occasions when I've felt a sense of menace attached to a spirit. They don't come through to scare or hurt us. Our souls are pure. So when people like this lady ask me to come and get rid of a spirit, I always try to find out if there's a valid reason. In this case, there wasn't. There hardly ever is. There were no pots and pans flying through the air. No levitation or rotating heads. That stuff happens in Hollywood and stays in Hollywood. Don't get me wrong, I love a ghost film as much as anyone. I love a spooky movie, all the suspense and the scary music, but when you take away the special effects and the acting, ghosts aren't frightening at all. When you think how many buildings there are and the small percentage that are said to be haunted, you realize that ghosts are rare and we're lucky to get a glimpse of them. Seeing a ghost is like seeing a rare animal. It's an experience we are lucky to witness.

The word 'haunting' comes loaded with so many negative connotations. Most of the time, what people call a haunting is a residual presence, a stain left on the fabric of space and time by a person who once inhabited that space and held it dear. It's a harmless residue. With residual energy, the pattern is always the same. The ghost or apparition will appear at the same places at similar times of the day. They may just drift down a hall and then fade away. They may act as if they don't notice you. Other times, there may be a spirit in the property.

The common misconception is that a haunting is a spirit stuck between worlds, in limbo and unable to move on into the afterlife and into Heaven. The truth is that, usually, if a spirit appears regularly in the same place or in the same building, it's because that building holds a sentimental attachment for it. They come back because they love being there. They are drawn to the energy of the property. Every house is like a little time capsule. It has its own experiences and history, which are like stored energy. This explains why older houses always seem more prone to hauntings: they have been around long enough to build up a big store of energy. Every house has a feeling about it. Some feel cold and unwelcoming, while others are homely and comfortable. It's all about the energy they have in them, and this is what attracts spirit. It's the magnetic effect I've talked about before.

As far as I'm concerned, spirits have just as much right to stay in a house as any of us do. In the afterlife, you don't need title deeds or a mortgage, you can move wherever you fancy, like a psychic squatter. So when someone like the woman I mentioned earlier gets in touch and asks me to cast a spirit back to the afterlife, I have to laugh. Some people have a very theatrical view of what I do. If it's a residual haunting, there's nothing I or anyone else can do about it. It's as much a part of the building as the foundations. And as for a spirit drawn to a property by its energy, well, even if I was some kind of supernatural bailiff I wouldn't trouble spirit if it was doing no harm. Only in the most extreme cases would I ever think about confronting a spirit.

I have to be honest and admit that I did once call in the services of an exorcist, but I really didn't want to. It was years ago, and I called him in to deal with a spirit in a house I was living in with John and the kids. The spirit, of a woman called Mrs Walters, was angry and impatient; it was as if she was always seeking attention. She would bang doors and slam windows and make a nuisance of herself. The children were terrified, and that's why she had to go. I tried talking to her, but it did no good. I hated having the exorcism, it went against so many of my beliefs, but I was left with no choice. On the whole, I respect spirit wholeheartedly, as should all of us.

I don't think we should encourage spirit in with uncontrolled séances and the like, and neither do I think we should try to get rid of them if they're not malevolent. If you have a spirit in your home, if there are strange, unaccountable noises from the plumbing (for some reason they seem to like kitchens and bathrooms), you should feel honoured. I have a theory about the kind of spirit that makes noises and moves things around. I don't think they do it to be bad and to misbehave and scare us; I think they need to be heard. I think they're desperately trying to attract our attention. I've felt it myself on stage when I have spirits lined up trying to come through. They butt in, push me and tug at me. They just want to get their messages across. If you live in a house or, rather, share one with a spirit, and it really, truly troubles you, if you can't live with it and accept it for the miracle that it is, often all you have to do is acknowledge the spirit. Just talk to it, tell it you're scared and ask it to go away. That usually does the trick.

Crazy as it sounds, you don't need a qualification in ghost-hunting to make yourself heard. You don't need a special laser zapper like they have in the movies. All you have to do is say loudly and clearly, 'I'm really scared, and I feel uncomfortable. Please could you stop.' I bet once you do that you'll have no more problems.

The Man in the Cupboard

When I was a child, there were ghosts everywhere. Everywhere I went was haunted because I had an unobstructed view of spirit. I hadn't worked out how to control my ability, so I couldn't close them off. So at home, in nursery and at school there were faces I saw all the time. They were the ghosts that haunted the nooks and crannies of my world. One of them was at my primary school. I could only have been six or seven. The school is still there today, in a corner of south-west London. It's a huge, imposing Victorian building, a very old-fashioned school set over five floors. The building would be classed as historic now. It still has those big sash windows the teachers have to open with a hook on a long pole. Inside it was a warren of corridors and staircases. When I was little, it seemed like a maze. Trying to negotiate your way around the place was a lesson in itself.

We had art classes up at the top of the building. The roof space had been converted, so we were up in the gods, with views out over south London. The room seemed enormous to me then. We'd stand at wooden easels which were lined up in rows and use blocks of watercolour paint. Each child would have a sheet of paper, a set of paints, a brush and a jam jar full of water. Right little Vincent van Goghs we were, our little faces screwed up in concentration as we created our works of art. Because we were in the eaves, there were lots of shadowy corners, and some of them had been made into cupboards so there was enough storage space for all the art equipment.

In one of the cupboards there was a presence. It was a man. I used to go in there and talk to him. Sounds mad, doesn't it? But he was there every art lesson and, as far as I was concerned, he was my special friend. Whenever I was on monitor duty, I'd collect up all the pots and paints and paintbrushes for the teachers and go and stack them in the cupboard and talk to my friend. There was nothing threatening or scary about him. Yes, he was a ghost but, to me, at that age and having been used to my ability from birth, it just seemed natural. He was just one of the 'others'; one of the people only I could see. It felt very cosy and warm in the cupboard chatting to him.

The teachers just assumed I was a strange child with an overactive imagination. They would hear me muttering in the cupboard and call me out, assuming I was misbehaving. Inevitably, this lack of understanding on the part of the teachers got me in trouble. One day, when I had been too long in the cupboard, the stern art teacher shouted at me to come out. I'm not sure why I chose that particular day to stage a rebellion, but I decided I wasn't going to do what she said. I'm going to put my foot down and stay with my friend, I decided.

'Come out,' the teacher snapped, staring into the gloom.

I refused.

Then the man said something odd to me.

'Tell her you were born on a bus.'

I didn't have a clue what he meant, but it sounded like a good idea. So I told the teacher I was born on a bus and

I wasn't coming out. The man giggled and urged me to say it again. I think he was feeling the mischievous energy and enjoying it. I repeated the words and the teacher became even more annoyed.

'You weren't born on a bus,' she said. 'You're just like your mother. I know all about her and the type of woman she is.'

That was it. When you're a child, the thing you cherish most in your life is your parents, and woe betide anyone who says anything bad about them. I was particularly protective of my mum because she'd had such a hard time. She had me when she was sixteen, which was very young, even in those days. And she'd married young and then got divorced, which was seen as even worse. It was taboo back then. But she refused to be stuck in an unsatisfactory marriage. She left him, and that made her a black sheep.

Now this annoying teacher was bringing Mum into our little set-to and I was livid. I was only little, I wasn't articulate or intelligent enough to argue with her rationally, so I just carried on repeating what the spirit told me to say.

'I was born on a bus, I was born on a bus,' I sang sarcastically.

The teacher had had enough after that. I felt a hand grab my foot and I was dragged out and torn a strip off in front of the rest of the class. I didn't care. I knew I had really riled the teacher and that was victory enough for me.

It took many years before I actually found out what that spirit was telling me that afternoon.

I wasn't born on a bus at all, I was born in hospital, but I was talking to my mum, Beryl, one day many years later when I was a teenager, and she was telling me about the day she realized she was pregnant. She was in her last year at school, just a girl herself, and she was terrified. The implications of being pregnant at that age were huge. She was unmarried, and the only way out if you were pregnant out of wedlock in the fifties was to get hitched: to have a shotgun wedding.

Mum had a gigantic decision to make and was in a complete daze. She told me she got on a bus and stayed on it as it drove around London, staring out the window but not focusing on anything, just trying to work out what she was going to do. She stayed on the buses all day, thinking to herself, 'I'm having a baby.'

When she told me this, I immediately remembered that day back in the art room at school and realized that must have been what the spirit was telling me about.

A short while ago, over fifty years since I had last set foot in the building, I had the opportunity to go back to the school while filming my show, *Psychic Sally: On the Road*. There were still reports of spirit activity going on in the same room and I was invited back to investigate. It all felt so strange walking back through the corridors of my childhood. The chairs and desks all seemed so dinky. But the building still had that feel about it. I was overcome with nostalgia. If anyone ever gets the chance to revisit their school, I'd wholeheartedly recommend it. The memories that came flooding back left me with a smile on my face all day long.

But I wasn't there for a trip down Memory Lane. I was shown up to the attic room, which is now a computer room – an 'IT suite', in modern language. Of course, it had all changed. The easels and paints had long gone, but the cupboards in the eaves were still there, and immediately I was drawn to the energy emanating from the one I had shut myself into all those years before.

'Oh my God, he's still in there,' I said. All the memories came rushing in and I was overwhelmed. I realized that the spirit had been pivotal in the way I see the world and use my gift.

I spoke to the school cleaner, Walter, and he told me that he was always experiencing unexplained things in the room. Just a few days before I visited, he had been working in the room late at night and felt someone walk past him. He said he had become so used to it that it didn't bother him any more.

And that is a good lesson. That spirit in the attic, that ghost, isn't there to scare anyone. He is part of the furniture, part of the building. Why would anyone want to send him packing?

Meeting the Ancestors

I love hearing people's ghost stories. It validates what I do. Whenever someone comes up to me and starts to explain that their home or workplace is haunted, I know that spirit is doing its job, interacting with us and looking over us.

I suppose when you're a doctor, people are always telling you about their ailments. Well, when you're a psychic, people are always telling you about their ghosts. And because I tour the country and meet so many people, I hear more ghost stories than anyone. From this unique vantage point, I can confirm that the country is well and truly haunted.

I've only got to walk into an old building and my psychic antennae start to twitch. Just recently, I was in Scotland having my hair done in a hairdresser's in Aberdeen. As I sat in the chair having my roots touched up, I felt an energy below my feet. If they haven't got a basement, the building is on top of a burial ground, I thought to myself.

I asked the lady who was doing my highlights if there was a basement underneath us, and she confirmed that the property did have a cellar. It was used as a stock cupboard, and one of the workers had run up the stairs in fear one day, having seen a vision of a little girl staring at her through the gloom.

I reassured the owner that there was nothing to be

scared of. That's what I always do when people tell me about hauntings: try to reassure them. It's about education. We need to try to coexist with spirit, not be fearful of it.

On that trip, I got the chance to have a little delve into my ancestry and discovered that, way back, several generations ago, my family originated from Scotland. My mother's maiden name was Cummings. Thanks to a clan tartan shop in Aberdeen, I discovered that the name Cummings means 'bent' or 'crooked'. I had to laugh. Given my family background, it seemed apt. The Cummings clan were also stonemasons. They built castles all over Europe, and while I was in the area I decided to visit one of the castles they would have helped build for a spot of ghost-hunting. I was performing at a show in the town and had some spare time so it was like a busman's holiday.

Even from the outside, the thirteenth-century castle looked imposing. With its turrets and battlements, it wouldn't have looked out of place in a Harry Potter movie. Inside, I immediately picked up on the building's atmosphere. In the entrance, I saw a lady dressed in a grey and blue taffeta dress. I explained what I had seen to a smartly dressed curator and she confirmed that she too had had a similar sighting in another part of the castle.

'I sense the name Alice or Alec,' I told her.

She believed I was picking up the lady of the house, who had been married to the laird. His name was Alexander, and she was called Anna.

I was taken upstairs to see a painting of the lady whose spirit I had picked up.

Then I saw him.

'Don't move,' I told the guide. 'But standing in the room

behind you, in front of a white door, there is a gentleman. He's dressed in a black waistcoat and is wearing black trousers cut off at the knee.'

He vanished as we walked into the room. The guide explained that the door he had been standing in front of led into a part of the house dating from the fifteenth century and into the laird's office and library.

We stepped through it into an amazing library room stocked to the ceiling with beautiful leather-bound books. And there, in pride of place on the far wall, was a painting of the man I had seen staring at me. He was wearing exactly the outfit I had described, except you couldn't see whether his trousers were knee length; the painting stopped at his knees.

'That's him,' I said. 'That's exactly who I just saw.'

It was as if the lady of the house had greeted me downstairs and he had called me into his study. It was wonderful. The house was alive.

But not everyone gets as excited as me when they see a ghost. Understandably, it frightens many people. It shouldn't, because spirit comes to us with love and openness 99 per cent of the time. In fact, I've had evidence before of spirits coming back to give reassurance when they have inadvertently scared someone.

One evening, I was standing on stage towards the end of a show and was aware of the energy of an elderly man who had been waiting on the periphery of my psychic vision for some time. It was as if he was allowing other spirits through before him. But with just ten minutes or so to go, he came forward, and I picked up the names 'Sid' and 'Sian'. He had a message: 'They saw me last week and someone screamed. She knew it was me,' he said.

I relayed this to the audience, and a nice-looking young girl stood up. She could have only been a teenager.

'I'm Sian,' she said. 'And my granddad is Sid. He's in spirit.'

I explained to her that Sid was telling me that someone felt they had seen him and that they were frightened by his presence. He was coming through because he wanted them to know that he hadn't meant to scare them.

'Does this make sense to you?' I asked.

She explained that, two weeks before, she'd been in bed asleep and had woken to see a shadow passing down the landing. It had shaken her. It was Sid, and he had come back to apologize and to reassure her.

Sid hadn't meant any harm when he showed himself to Sian and, once she realized that, after I had spoken to her, she was overcome with emotion.

Often it's the young who are the most accepting of ghosts. They are much more in touch with their intuitiveness and more open to spirit. It all goes back to my valve theory. If you haven't heard it, here it is:

I believe we all have a valve in our head that opens and closes and lets in psychic energy. It's the part of our mind that connects us to the other world, to the supernatural. When we are born, the default setting of that valve is 'open'. We are supposed to connect with spirit and the world around us. The psychic energy is everywhere and connects us all. It explains those common incidences in life where you think of someone you haven't thought about for ages and, within a few hours, they phone. It explains why two people sometimes think or say the same thing at the same time. It explains déjà vu. In children and animals, the valve is open but, as we get older, as we get bogged down in logic and facts and reasoning, that valve starts to close.

I'm lucky. When I was a child, Nanny Gladys had the ability and, because of that, my mum never encouraged me to close myself off to spirit; she actually encouraged it and let me develop it. Sometimes, a child's ability to be open to spirit is not a good thing – but only rarely.

Some friends of ours in the north of England once lived in a beautiful old stone farmhouse with their severely autistic son. He was unable to communicate and had not spoken properly for years. John and I visited them once and I felt a chill about the house. Although on the surface it was beautiful and full of character and had been reno-vated to a high standard, underneath, on a psychic level, it was cold. It was inhabited by one of those rare bad spirits. And as I walked through the house I felt it strongest in their son's room. I was certain that through being so close to this bad energy, and particularly because of his condi-tion, their son was being adversely affected by it, and when they eventually decided to move I was hugely relieved.

Often though, children are much more accepting of spirit than we are and, because of that, they can tend to be the focus of attention in a haunted house. My grandson Arthur has a ghost in his bedroom. It throws balls at him sometimes. He thinks it's hilarious.

I met a lady once who told me that her son would often talk about his great-grandmother and how, no matter where he dozed in the house, he would always wake and see her floating above him. Now, most people would scream if they woke up and were confronted by the image of an elderly lady in a flowing dress with a shock of white hair levitating up above them, but this boy thought it was great. She was there because she wanted to be with her family. Perhaps we should all try to be a bit more childlike when it comes to ghosts. They just want to be loved.

Guardian Angels

You hear a lot of talk about angels. People love the idea of them. It's comforting to know that there are holy beings sent from Heaven to give messages and to guard us. The idea is that they are distinct from spirit. They are powerful and take a physical form. You can touch them; they are made of matter, not just energy and thought patterns. They are divine flesh and blood – and let me tell you: they exist.

They are incredibly rare, and seeing a real angel is one of the most breathtaking things you will ever be privileged to witness. I have seen four in my life, each time at a moment when I was in danger, and each time it blew me away.

So what are they? Well, I don't want to upset anyone, because there is a whole culture of belief that has grown up around the concept of angels. I often see features and articles in magazines which present them as pretty, dainty little entities that sit on your shoulder and proffer polite advice, like Tinkerbell in *Peter Pan*. That is a lovely interpretation of what an angel appears to be but, believe me, it's far from the truth. They are bloody awesome.

A real angel can be eight foot tall, and they are usually men. I don't know why that is. They have white wings folded in an arc behind their backs which make them appear even taller. They tower above you, and they're bathed in a divine light, a soft, ethereal glow. And now I'm going to say something else that sounds really nutty. Their skin is silver, and they dress in silver. They have wide eyes, like deep, dark pools, and their eyes are hypnotic. You know the way aliens are portrayed in movies sometimes, as tall, thin beings? They look a bit like that. They aren't scary: they're calm and powerful. You don't feel frightened around them, but you do feel a huge amount of reverence.

The first time I saw an angel I was just a little girl. I must have been about nine or ten. I was crossing the main road near our house in Fulham with my sister and one of her friends, Sylvia. I know it must have been many years ago, because there were trolley cars going up and down the road. I was between my sister Gina and Sylvia, holding their hands, because I was the oldest. I was wearing a light white cotton dress and I remember edging out into the road to see if there were any vehicles coming. A trolley bus had stopped just in front of us, so I couldn't see clearly past it but I could see enough to think it was safe to edge out. Big mistake! As I stepped forward ahead of the other girls, I walked right into the path of a motorbike.

It caught my dress, and I can remember being jolted forward like a rag doll and then rolling across the road, right into the path of the oncoming traffic. I was injured quite badly, I had deep cuts on my hip and my arms, and was so dazed I couldn't get up. I just lay there looking at these cars coming towards me. And that's when he came, the angel. He was a very, very tall man, and I lay there blinking up at him as time seemed to slow down. He was glowing; his face was expressionless. He bent down, and I had the sensation of being lifted up and supported across the road to the other side. It all happened slowly and calmly, and I felt his reassuring arms holding me carefully.

The moment I reached the other side and he let go of me, it was as if the world snapped back to normal speed. The cars that were heading towards me zoomed past just inches away, sounding their horns. Witnesses said I got up and walked away in the nick of time – they hadn't seen what I had. I'll always remember that strong feeling of reassurance as those arms lifted me. I'm not sure, but I reckon it was very similar to what it feels like when we die and our souls rise from our bodies.

Several years later, we were on holiday, camping in Cornwall. Foreign travel then was a rarity – there was no such thing as a package tour – and to normal people like us Spain was as alien as the moon. Holidays, if you had them at all, were taken in the UK. If you lived in London, you might go to Brighton or Worthing, or to the country in Kent or Sussex. If you were being really exotic, you would go to Wales, where they even spoke another language. And if you wanted somewhere far flung you'd go to Devon or Cornwall, which is where we ended up most years.

We went with another family who lived in the same road. The dad was called Denny. He was a fireman, and a bit of a hunk as far as the female community in Waldemar Avenue was concerned. My mum used to like it when Denny came on holiday with us because, when the weather got hot, Denny used to take off his T-shirt. He was a bit of a show-off was Denny and, although he didn't admit it, you could tell he knew that taking his top off got the ladies hot and bothered, so he did it every opportunity he could get.

This particular holiday, I was in my swimming cossie braving the Atlantic, playing in the waves. God knows how, but kids don't seem to feel the cold. Denny came splashing in and I swam out with him into the deeper water. I wasn't a bad swimmer at all – I used to go every week back home – but a little way out I felt an undercurrent, and the next minute I was under a wave trying to get to the surface. The more I tried, the further the surface seemed to be. I can remember it so vividly. I was underwater, thinking, I'm ten years old, I'm going to die. I wasn't even panicking; I just thought, This is it for me, it's all over. And then he appeared: a man floating through the water. He was glowing and – don't laugh – he was wearing white underpants. He looked like a luminescent Man from Atlantis. I knew it wasn't Denny, because Denny was wearing red swimming trunks. And this man's eyes looked huge, like the eyes of one of those fish that live in the dark at the bottom of the ocean. As I was repeating 'I'm going to die,' in my mind, I heard another voice: his. It said: 'No you're not. I'm here.' And then I felt myself being pushed up with great force to the surface. I must have looked like a salmon jumping out of the water. I gasped for breath, and the force of the push sent me floating to the shallows, where I dragged myself on to the sand, coughing and spluttering.

I told my parents that I had nearly drowned, and that a man had thrown me to the surface. They said it must have been Denny, but he had been nowhere near me, and when he eventually swam to the beach to see what all the fuss was about, he said that it definitely hadn't been him. The only explanation he could offer was that maybe there was some kind of current or wave under the water that had caught me and pushed me up. There was a rock in the water near where it happened, and my mum made my dad swim round it to see if he could see anyone. There wasn't a soul there.

The third time I encountered an angel was in hospital. I was heavily pregnant with my middle daughter, Rebecca. I used to suffer from pre-eclampsia which, if you're a mum, you will know is potentially very dangerous for you and your baby. It's characterized by blood pressure problems and fluid retention and it affects the blood flow through the placenta. Because of the problems I was having, I went into labour at thirty-two weeks.

One of the outcomes of pre-eclampsia is that you have very small babies, because the placenta itself is small. When I started having early contractions I went to Queen Charlotte's Hospital in London, where the midwives realized that I was two centimetres dilated. They checked Rebecca's size and realized she was far too small to be born. By this stage, I was in a real state. The contractions were very painful, and there were loads of doctors around me trying to work out how to stop the birth.

One of them leant into me and said, 'We have to give you this drug. If you have your baby now, it will die. Its lungs are not properly formed. It won't be able to survive.'

This was thirty years ago, and care for premature babies was not like it is today.

In my delirious agony, I was begging the doctors to let me have the baby, but they managed to calm me down and reassure me that this drug they were talking about would be the best and safest option. Then they explained that its one side effect was that when it went in it would make my heart race. Well, they weren't kidding. Seconds after the needle left my arm I felt my chest start to thump and my head go light.

'I'm going to die,' I croaked as I started to lose consciousness. As everything started to go fuzzy, I became aware of a very tall man. I thought he was another doctor. He put his hand in my chest, and I felt that familiar, otherworldly calm. I felt my heart slow and relax and the panic wash away.

He's a good doctor, I thought to myself. Then, just before I fell into one of the most restful sleeps of my life, I saw the wings folded behind him.

When I woke many hours later, my baby was safe and still in my tummy where she was supposed to be, and I was stable. I asked a nurse who the tall doctor was and whether hallucinations were a side effect of the medication I had been given. She didn't know any tall doctors and said the medication was not psychotropic in any way.

The last time I saw an angel was the most bizarre. It wasn't too long after the hospital drama. Rebecca was a baby and I was on my own with her in our house. We were eating lunch in our tiny little kitchen in New Malden, Surrey. She was in her high chair eating soft, mashed-up Weetabix. She was slopping it everywhere, just getting used to using a spoon, and I was eating a sandwich, laughing at her. As she pinged a huge splodge of it at the fridge, I guffawed and immediately started wheezing. A lump of the beef sandwich I was eating had gone down my throat. I was choking. Try as I could, I just couldn't cough it back up, and the veins in my throat started to bulge as I clawed at my neck and began to panic. The weird thing was that it wasn't so much the thought of dying that terrified me, it was the knowledge that if I keeled over there and then, my baby would be trapped in her high chair all day until John got home.

Now, if you think the last three examples are odd, wait until you hear this. Just as I was starting to black out, I felt myself being picked up from behind. I saw two strong, glowing arms wrap around my chest and then I felt myself being slammed down on to the kitchen table with such force and accuracy that the bit of beef sandwich that was killing me dislodged itself from my throat, flew out of my mouth and landed splat in the middle of Rebecca's bowl. An angel had performed the Heimlich manoeuvre on me!

I lay there stunned, sucking in air. Rebecca started giggling. She thought it was hilarious. She'd just seen her mummy launch across the room and land on the table.

As they are so rare, I don't come across many people who share my experiences. I've spoken to clients who believe they have seen an angel, but they are usually confusing angels with spirit. There is no physical dimension to the entities they describe. I have no idea why I have been protected by them so many times. Maybe someone or something believes I have a gift worth protecting. Who knows?

The only time I can really say I heard of another case of angel intervention was when a friend and client of mine fell ill several years ago. To protect her privacy, I'll call her Joanne. She lived in a remote house in the Welsh countryside with her two children. She started to come to me when she lived in London and was having relationship problems with her husband. After they divorced, we remained friends, and she moved away to make a fresh start on her own with the kids. I often worried about her, because she seemed so fragile sometimes. The breakdown of her marriage hit her hard, and it was many months before she found her feet again. Joanne was a good, kind soul, and I went to visit her one weekend. As we sat in her kitchen on the Saturday afternoon sipping coffee, she told me that she had recently been very unwell.

'I thought I was going to die, Sal, I really did,' she explained.

She had caught flu, the proper kind that knocks you for six, and because she was so emotionally drained she couldn't fight it and it developed into an even worse chest infection. She was unable to look after her children and was terrified they would catch the illness too, so they went to stay with their dad while she was laid up alone getting worse and worse.

'I was in bed, panting and drenched in sweat,' she recalled, 'and then I had the strangest experience. This man came to me. He was huge, with these amazing big eyes. He had wings tucked behind his back, Sal. Can you believe that?'

I nodded, smiling to myself.

'And then he touched me. He just laid his hand on my chest, and I felt so calm I drifted off to sleep. I was out for a couple of days, but I woke up once and he was sitting on a chair looking at me. He looked funny because his legs were so long, stretched out in front of him. It looked as if he was sitting on a child's seat. When I finally woke properly after a couple of days, I was right as rain. And I felt totally refreshed.

'I think I must have been hallucinating, because the

weirdest thing was – and I know this sounds mad – he was wearing a silver suit. What's that all about?'

She was laughing at just how silly it all sounded.

'I reckon it means you've got a guardian angel,' I told her, smiling.

The Man from the Dark Side

The world is made of opposites: light and dark, men and women, positive and negative. That seems to be the natural order of things. And so, inevitably, because we have such pure goodness in life – such as angels – we also have pure evil

And, thankfully, while pure good is rare, so is pure evil. I've only come face to face with it on a few occasions, and I'll never forget it.

The most disturbing energy I ever came in contact with seeped out of a man who called for a reading many years ago.

John would usually take the bookings and deal with my diary in those days but, on this particular day, I happened to be walking past the phone when it rang so I picked it up.

'Sally Morgan?' came a heavy American accent from the receiver. He spoke in a deep drawl. He only said the two words, but I sensed a mocking tone in them.

'That's me,' I said, trying to sound chirpy. I could already sense something bad around this person.

'So you're the lady who can speak to the dead, are you? I want to come and see you,' he said.

'OK. Can I ask where you got my details from?' I always asked this question. It helped filter out the undesirables.

He mentioned the name of a client, a reputable woman I'd been seeing for some time, so I agreed to take the booking. As I gave him a time and asked his name, an image of a battleship floated into my mind.

'Mr Ship,' he said.

I giggled.

'What are you laughing at?' he snapped.

I was taken aback.

'I'm so sorry,' I apologized. 'I wasn't laughing at your name. It was just that, as you said your name, I saw a boat.'

He sneered audibly and hung up. I shivered as a chill ran down my back.

I forgot all about the unnerving man until the day of his appointment a couple of weeks later when I was looking in the diary and saw his name. He was due at 4 p.m., and in the hours before he arrived I felt unsettled. He had such a bad air around him on the phone that I shuddered to think what he might be like in the flesh.

I found out when, dot on four, there was a deep rumble outside the house. I peeked through the net curtains and saw a huge black Harley-Davidson screech to a halt on the kerb outside. The man who got off it was over six feet tall and stocky. He wore black boots, black jeans, a black leather jacket and a black helmet with the black visor pulled down. I shivered as he trudged up the driveway and knocked heavily on the door.

I opened the door and tried to smile sweetly and welcome him in, although by now I knew it had been a huge mistake to accept his booking. I could feel the evil on him oozing from every pore. He was infected with bad energy, and it was eating him like a cancer. He knew I knew he was evil and, as I opened the door to him, I was met with a torrent of abuse as he pushed it himself.

'You whore, you bitch,' he yelled.

The hallway led to the kitchen at the back of the house, and John was at the sink, doing the washing-up. He heard the commotion and ran to the front of the house. I'll never forget it, he had suds all up his arm. He looked like someone from the Fairy Liquid adverts.

'What's going on?' he shouted over the din.

By now I could feel the evil energy the man had brought with him creeping into my mind. Awful images of his past were flashing into my head. I knew he had been in the Marines and that he had done despicable things. I saw him trying to strangle a young woman on a sofa.

'He tried to kill someone, John, he's evil. Get him out!' I cried.

The man still had his helmet on and, although I couldn't see his eyes, I could feel them boring into me, as if he was probing me to see if I really could do what I said I could, to see if I really did have the gift. I don't know why, but I felt that was why he was there; he had been drawn to me for some reason, and his bad energy felt like it was probing my mind. As hard as I could, I tried to force it out.

John grabbed him and bundled him to the door. Then he did something strange. He threw a cheque at me – my fee – and screamed for me to take it.

'I can't take his money, John,' I screamed. And as the man was pushed back out the door John reached down, picked up the cheque, screwed it up and threw it after him. I slammed the door and leant against it, breathing heavily. I don't why I needed to give his money back, or why he was now eager to take it, but my intuition told me that under no circumstances should I enter into anything that could be seen as a contract of service with this man.

Outside, the man was still shouting abuse and banging on the door. For one comic moment he lost his keys and started to check all the pockets and zips in his jacket before he found them. Then he jumped on his motorbike and screamed off.

I was shaking and in shock. The whole episode lasted less than a minute but it has remained imprinted on my memory to this day.

Once I calmed down, I wanted to know who or what this man was and where he had come from, so I began to make enquiries.

I called the client who had supposedly recommended me to him and told her about the awful experience. She could not recall ever meeting the mysterious Mr Ship. Well, he's not the kind of person you could forget.

She said she would ask her friends and, a few hours later, she called me back.

'My son was in a pub a few weeks ago,' she explained. 'He was chatting to one of his friends and mentioned that I had seen a psychic and told him some of the uncanny things you had come out with during our readings. As he was talking about you, he felt a tap on his shoulder, and when he turned around there was a huge American man behind him who demanded your details. He was very gruff and rude. My son gave him your name. He must have looked up your number.'

So that's how Mr Ship came to know of me. But I was still none the wiser as to where he had come from and what had made him so evil.

My client continued, 'After the man had left, my son asked around the pub to see if anyone knew the bloke. And a couple of people did. They said he was a former US Marine but he had been kicked out of the service, he'd been court-martialled and dishonourably discharged,' she explained.

'What for?' I asked.

'He was obsessed with the occult,' she answered. 'He was practising black magic.'

Normally, I'm the eternal optimist. I try to see the good in everyone I meet, because I do believe that in all of us there is some good. Actually, I'll rephrase that, I *did* believe that there is some good in everyone – until I met Mr Ship. There was nothing good about him, and any love that might have been in his soul had gone, eaten away by the negative energy he had dabbled in when he started playing with black magic. Thank God that to come across evil as pure as that is incredibly unusual. Most of us will never have to face it. As for what will happen to Mr Ship's soul when he dies, I can honestly say I do not know; I'm not sure he even has a soul left. All I can say is that, even though he terrified me and still haunts my dreams some-times, I actually pity him.

The Confusion of Sudden Death

I could see him in front of me: he wasn't quite solid; he flickered like a desert mirage. His energy pushed to the front of my mind and he appeared in human form. He was stooped forward and his head was buried in his hands. He didn't want to show his face. I sensed something awful behind those closed fingers.

In my mind, the audience melted away behind him as I focused in on him. I could hear him crying in frustration. Through the sobs, I caught his name. Neil.

I threw it out to the audience.

'He's a lovely fella,' I told them.

An elderly lady in a crocheted yellow top stood up nervously. My instinct was alive and it told me that this man on stage with me was here to give her a message.

As she rose, through the man's muffled cries, I heard another name.

'Marie?' I offered. She nodded her head. It never fails to amaze me how accurate the names have become over the last few years. Mostly, now, when they come through, they're crystal clear. In an audience of over a thousand people, I had paired up the right person with the correct spirit, and all it took was two names. Marie explained that Neil was her nephew. He had died thirty-three years ago in an accident.

The image of the prone man that I was being shown was both disturbing and sad, and I knew I had to try to reassure this lady about what I was seeing. Neil was showing me himself in death, not as he was now; his afterlife form was energy and love. Marie appeared slightly dazed by the experience. It's not surprising, I suppose. All eyes were on her.

I started to explain to her.

'I get shown things they did just before they died. This is what he's showing me. I feel as if I have my head in my hands – does that make sense?'

She nodded.

Then I got the name June. Marie indicated the seat next to her.

'I'm with my sister. Her name is June,' she said. June stood up.

Something else was pushed into my mind: the number thirty.

'Was he thirty when he died?' I asked the two women.

'Twenty-nine,' June said. 'But he always used to joke and say he didn't want to reach thirty. As far as he was concerned, that was old.'

Joking or not, it seemed poor Neil's wish had, tragically, come true.

Although the detail Neil was giving me was perfectly clear, I felt a degree of confusion coming from him, and it was to do with his passing. It's not uncommon. When people die suddenly, especially in accidents, their last moments on earth plane are confused. Their earth bodies are not ready to shut down. I suppose it's the biological survival instinct we all have. They fight for life, and that's what I pick up when they show me their dying moments. Of course, once the soul is free from its earthly bonds, it's a different story and there is only tranquillity and calm. Neil's confusion wasn't indicative of what he was feeling in the afterlife. He knew where he was; he'd been there a long time. It was projected confusion: he was showing what he felt when he died. It was an added detail to the story he was building up to let us know who he was.

I tried to explain to his aunts.

'He's in a good place, and no harm is going to come to him. He is in Heaven and nothing could be better. His soul will be there for ever and he is waiting for everyone, but I sense confusion in his passing.'

Neil showed me aspects of his death. He was conscious but gravely ill. He was talking to a doctor. He was begging: 'You've got to help me, you can't let me die.'

I explained this to his aunts, and the images rang 100 per cent true with them and their recollections. He had been in an accident and was very badly hurt and, despite their best efforts, the medical experts who looked after him couldn't make him right. He died from terrible head injuries. That was why he was covering his face.

It's always difficult when spirits such as Neil come through, spirits who died suddenly or in tragic accidents. It's not that they carry a sense of injustice into the afterlife with them. They let go of that when they pass. But when they show scenes of their death they also usually pass on details of the injuries they suffered and the feelings and emotions they had too – the confusion, the frustration. I guess, as their deaths were the last point of reference they had on earth, those are the images and memories they use to let us know who they are.

For relatives, it can be tough to re-live the details but, if

I don't pass on the information as I'm hearing it, I'm not doing spirit justice. They come through and give their messages for a reason, harrowing or not, and although stark details about their final moments may be hard to bear, they certainly help pinpoint who the message is meant for.

Other times, spirit appears disorientated when it comes through, solely because of the process. This is especially the case during a live show. When there are so many messages flying around and so much psychic energy, it can be just as disorientating for me. Often they have to fight their way through a melee to make themselves heard.

It's these feelings of confusion and displacement that come through when I'm channelling the spirit of an accident victim that make sudden-death readings so intense. A little bit of their death rubs off on me.

Take choking, for instance. Having once nearly choked to death myself, I know exactly what an awful and frightening experience it is. So when, a few months ago, a spirit pushed through and I felt my throat tightening, I came out in goose bumps. I knew what that feeling in my windpipe meant and I knew what was about to happen.

As soon as she came through, I felt my throat constrict, and I doubled over.

My voice dropped a couple of octaves and became gruff. As in so many readings, I felt like a puppet with the spirit pulling the strings. All I could do was hang on for the ride.

The name came to me.

'Vy,' I said. 'And I have Wendy too.' I was punctuating my words with coughs and wheezes. 'I think there may have been a problem with her throat,' I said, clutching my neck and stating the bloody obvious.

A lady stood. 'Up here, Sally,' she called from the balcony. 'My mum's name was Sylvia, but her family called her Vy.' Once again the name was spot on.

'What's with the throat thing?' I spluttered.

The lady explained that her mum had choked to death on a sandwich and that, as she was wheezing her life away, her husband, who had made the sandwich, had grabbed her from behind and bent her over to try to dislodge the food. It made sense: that was why I began the reading bent double.

Once the grim truth of Vy's death had been established, she then showed me a peaceful seaside, with beautiful white sand and rolling waves. Her words resonated in my mind.

'She says that her soul is by the sea,' I told her daughter, frowning. 'What does that mean?'

The lady nodded with a smile and explained that her dad was buried by the sea in Musselburgh, Scotland. Vy was letting her family know that she was with her beloved husband.

What I didn't know at the time but learned later was that, as a psychic virgin, the woman whom Vy came through for had, up until that point, been unimpressed by my show and had decided to leave. She soon changed her mind when her mum came through. And what is even more amazing is the reason I think Vy decided to bend me over and choke me to get her daughter's attention. I found out later that the woman's brother, Vy's son, was terminally ill. Vy came through to show him and her family that there is life after death, that he had no need to be afraid. Now that is what I call devotion.

Death on New Year's Day

The truth about death is always painful. The bit afterwards is the happy ending. We have to go through the bad bit to get to the good, and some passings are worse than others. Why do some of us get to pass peacefully while others die in pain? Well, it's part of that bigger plan I'm always going on about. It's all part of what is orchestrated for us by the higher being. We can't all die happily in our sleep of old age; that is a luxury afforded only to the lucky few. Nature and supernature are inextricably bound together and, with so many human beings on the planet, there just wouldn't be enough space or resources to sustain everyone into old age. There needs to be variety in death just as there is variety in life.

That, of course, does not make it any easier for people who have lost loved ones in sudden tragic circumstances. The grief process in accidental deaths is so much harder to overcome because of the sense of shock. It amplifies grief; it makes it so much harder to accept death.

Throughout my career, I've been privileged to have been able to help people come to terms with the shock of sudden death, and that is why I carry on doing what I do. The messages are the key. Each one is totally unique; each bit of information is sent out across the great divide for a purpose. They are sent with love. Each one is like a PIN number, totally individual to the spirit that gives it and meant specifically for someone, for a specific reason.

More often than not the reason spirits give their messages is just to let a loved one know that their love survives death and that there is someone watching over them from the afterlife. Sometimes, however, the messages I receive and impart go beyond this. Spirits often have the capacity to right wrongs from beyond the grave, as I discovered at a show not so long ago.

I knew the death was tragic as soon as I felt the energy. The show was at a theatre in the south of England and, up until the message came through, it had been a light-hearted evening. As they often do, the spirits had been larking around and being mischievous.

But midway through the show, just after the interval, I felt a girl, a teenager, and there was tragedy surrounding her death.

Before I even saw or felt any concrete details, I warned the audience. The atmosphere where I was standing on stage changed suddenly. The room went quiet: everyone felt it.

'Oh dear,' I said. 'It's not all going to be fun, is it?' I was talking to myself but addressing the crowd. The first feeling I had was that the girl had taken her own life. I looked down at my feet and, instead of looking at my shoes on the black stage, I saw a pair of young feet in stilettos, walking on a railway line. The image just materialized in my head and I projected it on to my surroundings.

Initially, I was confused by what was appearing in my mind. Sometimes, when a spirit comes through, especially that of a young person, they don't get their words out in the right order, so I thought this girl was telling me she'd jumped in front of a train. She kept saying sorry. Usually, that's the first thing people who have taken their lives say when they come through. They want to apologize to their loved ones for the grief their actions have caused.

I tried to articulate to the audience what was going on in my head.

'I have a lady who took her own life. I think she wanted people to think it was an accident because there was a train involved.'

But I wasn't sure. Again, with such a violent and sudden death, I was picking up a degree of confusion. Then came the breakthrough. A name screamed in my mind: Liam.

As I told the audience, a girl in the audience shrieked.

'Hello,' she said, waving to attract my attention. There was urgency in her voice and I could tell she was desperate for the message. Spirit realized how anxious she was to connect, and the fog that had surrounded the reading earlier cleared in an instant.

The girl was flustered. She was a pretty young thing, no more than eighteen years old and she explained the relevance of what I was picking up.

'My best friend died on the train tracks when I was sixteen. My ex-boyfriend's brother was with her at the time – he's called Liam. When she fell, people started saying that he pushed her, and he never did. It caused him a lot of trouble.'

The story was as tragic as any I had heard and I started to see the dead girl's final moments. It was New Year's Eve and she was with a group of her pals. They had all been out. It had gone midnight and there were no taxis to be found, so the group decided they would walk home along the railway line. They assumed, it being late at night and there being no trains running, that the rails would be off. They were messing around, as teenagers do, and the girl, in her heels, lost her balance and fell. She hit the rail, which was live, and thousands of volts shot through her young body. She died instantly.

The image I was shown was horrific. I picked up that the poor girl was terribly burnt all down her left side, and her friend in the audience confirmed that that was the side that sustained the injury.

The girl in spirit was clearer now. She was apologizing to Liam.

'She's screaming, "Liam, I'm sorry." '

The girl confirmed that, since the fatal accident, Liam had been shouldered with a huge amount of grief. He'd always been tortured by the thought that maybe he could have done something to save her, and this feeling had been aggravated by the whispering campaign against him.

She also had another message for her friend.

'She says, "Don't forget me," ' I explained. 'She wants you to ring her friends and tell them to remember.'

'It's funny you should say that,' the girl replied. 'Every year on her birthday I always went round and visited her mum, and the first time I didn't was last year.'

The spirit was wistful now. 'Come and see me,' she was saying.

I told the girl in the audience that she would be able to find her friend at her old home with her mother: that's where her spirit would be waiting.

It was an amazing reading, and I was so happy I was

able to channel it. The spirit of this girl knew that her friend would be in the audience, and she chose to come through to send a message to Liam that she was sorry for the pain her death had caused him. That's another thing about spirits: they are selfless.

Just One Cornetto

One of the most comforting things I can give to families who have lost members through tragedy is the assurance that their dearly departed are not alone. We all have people waiting for us on the other side and we are all reunited with our loved ones in death. That knowledge alone has helped so many families heal the heartache.

Sadly, some families seem to get more than their fair share of tragedy. So many times at my shows I'll hear stories of mothers who've lost sons and husbands, and it makes my heart weep. They are such brave people to bear that grief and come in search of comfort and reassurance. One such mum came to a show in the north of England, and the message from her son was so loud and so clear it was impossible to get it wrong.

It started with three names, clear as a bell, echoing in my head one after the other:

James, Francis, Mary. As I said them, the spirit of the young man who was giving them to me was guiding me across the stage to a specific area of the audience. I pointed to a lady in a shiny jacket and glasses. I was a hundred per cent certain that the message was for her and was determined that she would take it. I wasn't going to let her hunker down in her seat and pretend this young man in spirit was nothing to do with her. It sounds mad, but that's what some people do sometimes. They're too embarrassed to stand up.

'James?' I asked, pointing at the space next to me on the stage where the man had appeared. The audience couldn't see him, but I could.

She nodded. 'And you're Francis?' I asked.

'No, but my daughter is,' she said, pointing to the younger lady sitting next to her. 'James was my son.'

'That's his sister,' I said, amazed at my own accuracy. 'What else did I say? Mary?'

The lady smiled and told me that was her name. There was no doubt at all that James had come to see his mum.

It transpired that James had died in a car accident. He had been driving through a rainstorm when his car hit a huge puddle and aquaplaned into the path of an oncoming car.

And James had not been alone.

Standing with him now on stage was another man. They were both the same age, in their late teens, and I could tell there was a vague family resemblance.

'There's a nineteen-year-old boy with him as well. He's called Paul.'

A shock of recognition shot through Mary.

Speaking into the microphone, she explained: 'That's his cousin in Canada. He died at a similar age.'

Now, I'm not one to blow my own trumpet, but credit where credit is due. There was absolutely no doubt about what I was picking up. Every name was spot on.

Paul had died in almost identical circumstances to his cousin. He'd been driving home and a blizzard had swept in, creating what they call a white-out, where the snow is so heavy all you can see is white. Paul didn't stand a chance. He couldn't see where he was going, crashed and was killed instantly.

The cousins were together in spirit. Geography doesn't matter on that plane. It made no difference that one cousin died in the UK and the other halfway across the world in Canada. What mattered was that, in death, they were together.

Then James did something really off the wall: he started singing. In my head I could see him standing there on stage with his cousin (who was grinning) and he was holding a pretend microphone to his mouth and singing. And not just any old song either. He was singing the jingle to the old Cornetto adverts. You know the one, it's sung to the tune of the Italian song '*O Sole Mio*'.

I took a deep breath.

'You're going to laugh now,' I warned. 'But he's doing this.' And mimicking what I was seeing in spirit, I held my own invisible mic, started swaying back and forth, and sang, 'Just one Cornetto, give it to me.' To be honest, I felt like a bit of an idiot.

But Mary didn't laugh.

'Oh my God,' she gasped.

'Is that what he used to sing?' I asked, amazed.

'We used to sell ice cream,' she said. 'We used to manufacture it. James worked in the family business at weekends when he came home from college, and he would sing, "Just one Cornetto".'

I couldn't believe it, and neither could the audience. They broke out into spontaneous applause.

Then James told his mum the most important message of all. He told her where she could be close to him.

'I am at home,' I repeated to her. 'I stand in the hall because I don't want to disturb you.'

Her Father was Waiting for Her

Tragedy doesn't always come in the form of sudden death of course. Sometimes it's the slowness of a death that causes the real heartache. In the years I've been a professional medium I've seen scores of people who are terminally ill, and I have nothing but admiration for them.

I can't begin to fathom what it must be like to know that you only have an allotted time left and that that time will be blighted by failing health and increasing pain. Yet the people I have met in this terrible situation always bear it with such courage and fortitude I'm humbled every time. Because, although we all may think there are advantages of knowing when you are going to die, there really aren't any. Ask yourself this: if you had the choice, how would you rather die, after a six-month illness during which you know you will never recover, or knocked over by a bus in a surprise accident? I know which one I'd choose. Give me the bus any day.

Terminally ill people come to me for a range of reasons, but the one thing they don't come for is because they want to be healed. I'm not a healer.

The main reason people come to me when they know they have only a limited amount of time left is for reassurance. They want to know that they will be moving on to better things, that once the pain passes they will be at peace and that someone will be there on the other side waiting for them. Sometimes they also want to know how best to spend the last months or weeks of life they have. I always give the same advice: spend it with the people you love.

A while ago I saw a woman who was dying of cancer. She had a family and a lovely home and life. She was a proud mum of two young children.

In an example of just how cruel fate can be sometimes, she first noticed an ache when she was gardening. She'd been leant over for hours in the garden tending her borders on a sunny day and developed an ache in her lower back. She was fit and healthy and just assumed she had overdone it. However, the pain didn't go away and, over the following few weeks, it became progressively worse. She went to her doctor. What followed is a common pattern. He first diagnosed a kidney infection and prescribed antibiotics and pain killers. Only after taking the tablets for several weeks without seeing an improvement did he send her to hospital. She had test after test and, only after months, with her pain becoming worse and worse, did they finally find out that she had cancer. It was in her liver, and it had spread from there to her bones. There was no hope. She underwent months of chemotherapy just to try to slow the disease down, but the treatment left her sicker than the cancer itself. In the end, knowing she was going to die, she took the decision to stop the chemotherapy and instead to make the most of the short time she had left. That's when she came to see me. She had just a few months left to live.

She was a lovely, inspirational woman, and she grasped those final months with both hands. She went on a family holiday to Thailand, a part of the world she had always wanted to see, and when she became too ill to travel I visited her at her home. I saw her the day before she died. She believed in Heaven and seeing me helped her. I was able to confirm to her that her relatives were there waiting for her. When I gave her readings, they were all there, giving me messages loud and clear and passing on information that only they would know, giving her encouragement and making sure she knew there was a life after death. I felt an obligation to be there for her. You just don't abandon people like that, not if you can do something so fundamental for them as to make sure they do not go in fear at the end of their days.

I picked up her father from the very first session, and he was there time after time, guiding her through her illness. She was an amazingly brave lady and I'm honoured to have known her. And I know her father would have been there waiting for her when she finally succumbed to her illness.

The Worst Word There Is

You know what I reckon one of the worst words in the English language is? It's not a swear word, but some people find it more offensive than any effing and blinding. The word is 'suicide'. It's a horrible word, and I'll tell you why. It comes loaded with too much baggage. It comes loaded with shame. I've never really understood why, but in some religions, such as Catholicism, it's seen as a sin. According to the Catholic Church, if you commit suicide, you don't get to go to Heaven. You are damned instead.

Rather than think about how desperately unhappy and confused suicide victims must have been to take their own lives, certain people in society frown on them and would punish them even more than they have already been punished.

I came across a very disturbing case at a show recently, and I'll have to change the details slightly here to protect the poor girl who was involved. She was only a teenager, and her father had killed himself.

It started with a photograph, just a small passport-sized one of a man's face. He looked around thirty-five. He had short dark hair, piercing green eyes and a strong jaw-line. There was just the hint of a smile flickering across his lips.

When I showed the picture to the audience, a woman and her daughter stood up. The girl, who was probably in her mid to late teens, was already crying and hugging her mum, who was comforting her. It must have been emotional for them, seeing his face projected on the screen on stage. My heart went out to her and I immediately said that, if she didn't want to stand, she didn't have to. I could feel the spirit of this man desperate to come through and connect with his wife and child, but I had a responsibility to the girl too and I was very aware of how emotional this reading could get. I had started seeing details of the man's death and I knew he had taken his own life.

'Do you want me to do this?' I asked the family. They nodded a yes.

I knew that the first thing I needed to do was to reassure them. The girl looked so sweet and innocent, and her life had been turned upside down and torn apart less than a year before, when her father had killed himself.

'All my life, I've seen people who have taken their own lives,' I explained to them. 'They are not punished. He is in a very, very good place.'

The man showed me the details of his death. He had hanged himself, but the detail didn't matter. What mattered was what he wanted to tell his family.

I could feel a deep regret emanating from him. Not regret about where he was – he was in paradise, he couldn't have been anywhere better. No, what was bugging this gentleman was the thought of the impact his death had had on his nearest and dearest, the woman and the girl standing in front of me now.

'This man knew that everyone was going to be furious and angry,' I said. His family nodded. That is the hallmark of a suicide. It leaves so many contradicting emotions. There is often deep resentment and anger from those left behind. They can't understand why their loved one left them. Mixed with all the normal feelings of loss and grief are those of shock and confusion and sometimes guilt – was it my fault? It's a destructive cocktail of feelings that leaves those left behind emotionally paralysed.

This man knew what he had done to his daughter and his wife and he wanted them to forgive him. He wanted to be allowed back into their lives.

'He says, "Am I allowed back home? Can I come home?" He knows that you shout at the top of your voice, "What have you done? Why did you go and leave me?"'

He was flooding me with his feelings, and I felt from him an acute sense of embarrassment. He just wanted to be accepted back in their lives in spirit. He wanted them to forgive him and lose their anger.

'He's embarrassed to come in the front door,' I explained. 'I'm telling him he can go home. You need to feel him there so that you can talk to him.' He showed me the family home, and it felt bereft and soulless.

'It's empty at the moment,' I told them.

Then he gave me the little girl's name and she began to sob. I knew that the message I was giving was incredibly important to that family at that time, and I knew it would help them. But I felt almost trapped standing there on stage with a girl crying in front of me. I wanted to stop the show and take her somewhere quiet and talk to her.

I focused everything on her, and met and held her gaze. There was just me and her in that room, as far as I was concerned.

'Your dad hasn't gone anywhere,' I explained to her. 'You put this lovely picture of your father in my basket and he came through for you. You have so many un-answered questions. All you need to know is that he is in Heaven. When we die we do not disappear. It is very con-fusing, sweetheart, because we know they are there, but we can't see them. But you know Daddy's here now and he watches over you. He's got permission to come in now and you'll feel him indoors. It will all be all right.'

I hope more than anything that the girl got comfort from my reading. Her daddy was there on stage, reaching out and trying to bridge the gap he had opened between them. There are few negative feelings in spirit, so it would be wrong to say he was regretful. He was, however, nos-talgic, and I felt a yearning from him that came from the deep love he had for his wife and daughter. It left a mark on me too. I was so emotional at the end of that reading I had what can only be described as an uncharacteristic rant. Everyone who knows me knows what an easy-going, happy-go-lucky person I am. And I love my work and take great pleasure in it. However, because there was a lit-tle girl involved and because I am a mother myself, I was overwhelmed and felt I needed to get my feelings off my chest. I wanted people to know that what I do, I do to help people, not to exploit them.

'It's not easy,' I told the audience. 'Some people will say of me, "Oh, she's got a tour, she must be coining it in." But I live in the same house I have for years, a three-bed-room semi. I'd like to see them come and do this and see what I get in my head every single day of my life. It's not a piece of cake, and there's a huge responsibility that goes with it that I still battle with.'

Now, at the beginning of this story I started by explaining

how 'suicide' is one of my least favourite worst words in the English language because it comes with so many negative connotations. Well, that lovely little girl hadn't told all her friends about how her daddy had died. And after she came to the show some kids she knew heard about it and they started teasing her. How can anyone be so cruel? It makes my blood boil just thinking about it. That, in a nutshell, is the negative power of suicide. As if that poor child had not gone through enough.

It's such a shame there is this stigma attached to suicide. It's unfair, and much of the time it's driven by ill-advised religious doctrine. Whenever I do shows in Ireland, I'm particularly aware of the sensitivities of the audience when it comes to a subject that is frowned upon by many people there. Often there will be a reluctance to take a message if it comes from someone who took their own life.

During one show there a few years ago, a boy came through to me. Immediately I felt a sharp pain in my neck and my head drooped to one side. I knew the boy had died of a broken neck and I knew he had hanged himself. He was calling for his mammy.

But no one was taking the message, no one would acknowledge it, yet the boy's energy was coming through loud and clear and he was even directing me to an area of the audience where he knew his mother was sitting.

You've probably worked out by now that the one thing that really winds me up is when people are in the audience and they know the message is meant for them but, for whatever reason, they refuse to take it. It's just plain rude. Those spirits have gone to a lot of effort to come through, and the least we can do is acknowledge them.

Well, you can imagine how I was feeling when I knew the mother of this boy was there but wasn't going to take the message from him because he had committed suicide.

I'm not letting this one go, I told myself, and I kept repeating what I was picking up. I addressed the section of audience the boy was directing me to.

'You must take this,' I implored and, finally, in the spotlight, a little lady put her arm up.

I felt sorry for her and reassured her that there is no shame in dying, however we pass. When she did open up, she took great comfort from the reading, and that was all her son wished.

If we took away the word 'suicide' and just referred to it as another form of death, we would ease so much suffering. I hope that one day the word 'suicide' will be as archaic as 'illegitimate'. When I was growing up, if your parents weren't married when you were born, you were illegitimate and there was a huge stigma attached to it. It was used as a label, a term of abuse. You don't hear it used like that now; it no longer has those connotations. It has lost its power, and that's what I'm hoping will happen to 'suicide'.

The problem is that we judge using the values we have acquired on earth plane. And they do not work in spirit. The reason many people and religions scorn suicide is because of the belief that all life is sacred, therefore, to take a life, including your own, is sacrilegious. But I've always argued that, if life was that precious, no one would ever die. It's the afterlife that is sacred, not life itself. Life is just a transition point in the journey, and to assume that when someone commits suicide they get punished for it on the other side is ignorance. I feel I can speak with some authority here, having been in contact with so many people who have taken their lives. I can honestly say that every one of them is at peace and, when they pass, they pass just like everyone else. They are met by loved ones, they are taken to a place of peace and love and they are not judged.

A Message of Reassurance

Without a doubt, suicide is one of the most distressing ways to lose a loved one. There is so often blame attached. If there is a note left explaining the reason why, it usually implicates people. We say people are *driven* to suicide, and in most cases it is other people who do the driving, usually unintentionally. It could be a former lover or a distant parent that leads someone to take their own life, and if a note detailing the reasons is left, those implicated are saddled with a lifetime of self-blame and regret. And because death is so final, that blame remains, festering inside.

The flip side is that, if someone takes their life and doesn't leave a note or a message, then there is doubt and confusion. Did they mean to kill themselves? If so, why? Whose fault was it? Suicide is like an atomic bomb. The blast sucks in so many other casualties and the fallout remains there for years and years. Sometimes it never gets washed away. Usually, people who commit suicide are so confused and distraught they can see no other way out and they're unable to consider the implications of their actions logically. It's only in the peace and tranquillity of the afterlife that they can assess the impact of their passing, and that's why one of the first things spirits who take their own lives want to say when they come through is 'sorry'.

I did one reading recently where those emotions of

regret and guilt had carried on for nearly thirty years until I became involved.

The dead man's name was Andrew. When he came to me and showed me how he'd passed, my heart felt like iron. He had been so, so sad. He was crying, and all hope had gone from him. His energy made me physically shake and shiver. This was how he was in his dying moments: confused, cold, desperate for peace, his life ebbing away. He found the peace he craved but he wanted to get in contact with someone he had left behind, a friend called Sally. I was reading for her. The first thing Andrew wanted to say to her was sorry.

'He wants to apologize. He says that he called you and left you a message before he died. He says that no one understood him. He was a very confused young man,' I explained to her as the message came through.

Sally confirmed that days before Andrew took his own life he had left a message on her answer phone, which she failed to return. He had died twenty-eight years ago, but she was still haunted by the guilt of that unreturned call. She had always wondered if, had she spoken to her friend, she may have been able to change what he'd done. He had gassed himself.

'I feel so guilty,' she said. 'If I had answered that message and gone to see him, maybe he wouldn't have done it.'

I reassured her.

'You mustn't feel guilty, he would have done it anyway. There was nothing you could have done to change what happened,' I told her.

Andrew was repeating the words 'Two days' over and over.

'Did they find him two days after his death?' I asked Sally.

She nodded, but explained that when the emergency services found Andrew he was unconscious but still alive. He died two days later in hospital and, throughout those forty-eight hours, Sally sat with him. He was telling her how much he appreciated her being there for him.

'Tell him I forgive him,' she told me.

I felt it then. It was like a change in the temperature; a thawing from both earth plane and spirit. Andrew and Sally had made their peace.

Of course, no one really considers all the implications when they commit suicide, unless of course we're talking about terminally ill people who arrange to take their lives (the practice of euthanasia). But these are rare cases. For me, being able to facilitate an exchange between a loved one and a suicide victim is one of the most rewarding aspects of my work. I get to see instant results, as in the case of Sally and Andrew. Questions are answered and forgiveness is granted. Sometimes it feels like unblocking a pipe – as if I was some kind of psychic plumber! Once that blockage has been removed, the process of grief can flow freely again.

Tying Up Loose Ends

I could see the pills scattered around the stage; only it wasn't a stage in my mind. I was in a bedroom. There were scores of them; and they had spilled from upturned medicine bottles. There were several different types and they were all different colours: bright reds and yellows and blues and greens. They could almost have been sweets. And I could smell booze too. It stung my nostrils.

The audience was oblivious to all this. It was a scene I was being shown in my psychic mind. There was a lady there in the room, writhing on the bed, grabbing handfuls of pills and shoving them in her mouth, washing them down with some kind of strong spirit. It was a suicide, and the lady in spirit seemed distant, as if she was far away. I shivered. Then I saw a house. I began to explain to the audience what I was experiencing.

'I have a lady here, and I can smell alcohol. There are lots and lots of pills all over a bed and on the floor, and she's trying to grab them.

'Now I'm looking at a house. It's very distinctive: it has a large bay window, which is very low, coming down almost to the ground at the front. The house is painted a yellow or lemony colour. It's Victorian or Edwardian.'

Then a name. 'Susan?'

As I walked across the stage, I saw a hand go up. A woman in a pink jumper and glasses stood.

I asked her what I had said that resonated with her, and she explained that her sister had taken her own life and that the house I was describing sounded identical to the house where she had died. The departed had lived in New Zealand and the woman now speaking to me had gone to visit the house after her sister's death. The description I had given was uncannily accurate. The lady also mentioned that she had been talking to her sister's best friend that day, and her name was Sue.

With the connection made, the lady in spirit repeated her message. 'I'm sorry, I'm sorry,' she kept on saying, again and again.

'She tells me, "I didn't want to drink any more, I didn't want that every day,"' I explained. I could sense that her last days had been lived in a state of utter confusion and desperation. She had felt like a cornered animal, trapped by her addiction to alcohol. But what came through was a feeling of love for her sister. She wanted to make things right.

'She loves you,' I explained. 'But she couldn't go on with her head in the state it was in.'

That's all she had needed: to help her sister understand why she did what she did.

Only a few days after this woman came to me I was giving a personal reading and felt the same energy as another suicide victim came through. The sadness and the guilt marked it out.

Now I don't want you thinking that those are the feelings the people who commit suicide take with them into eternity, because they are not. What they do is show me what they felt as they passed. They channel those feelings through me to allow themselves to be recognized.

The spirit came to me from a photograph the lady had brought with her. It showed a smiling man in his forties sitting in an armchair holding a fluffy black dog.

'There is tremendous guilt connected to this passing,' I told the lady. She confirmed that the man, her uncle, had taken his own life.

The guilt I felt was almost overpowering. It washed aside all the other emotions I had been picking up. This man wanted forgiveness. He wanted it understood that he had never meant to upset any of his family, and he wanted his niece to know that he'd felt he had no choice.

'It had to be that way,' I explained to her. She nodded. She understood what her uncle was saying.

It's comforting sometimes that just a small interaction, a short connection between the living and the dead, can heal doubt and sadness. By making contact and by sharing messages and loving energy, spirits allow us to move on and tie up loose ends.

Other times, they come through with very specific requests. In another recent reading I was shown the photo of a lovely young teenager. She was probably around fourteen years old, she had clear olive skin and dark hair. But behind the smile in the photo, I sensed suffering. She appeared to me, and I knew she had taken her own life. She had hanged herself. The receiver was a distant family member, a middle-aged woman who had come to see me because of problems in her immediate family, but she had shown me a picture of this girl and now I was picking up a message from her. I felt an urge from the spirit: for some reason, this girl was saying that she wanted to return home.

I tried to explain this to the woman.

'I feel like I want to say, "Come back." Did she go abroad?'

The woman confirmed that the girl had died in Lanzarote.

'Is she buried there?' I asked.

'Oh my God, yes she is,' the woman replied. It transpired that the young girl had gone to the island to live with her mother, who was British and had emigrated. But now her mother had moved back to the UK and her daughter's body remained in the Canaries. The girl was passing a message to the receiver in the hope it would get to her mum.

'She wants to come back with her mother,' I explained.

Graham

Taking your own life seems alien to most of us, doesn't it? Thankfully, most of us have lives that are nice and stable and so we can't understand how anyone can be driven to such desperation that death becomes a valid option. Perhaps that's why suicide is such a misunderstood death. It seems illogical – after all, we're born with a survival instinct. Something must go terribly wrong for people to be able to turn that instinct off.

There are patterns, though. Most suicides are carried out by men. I think that is because us women are much more in tune with our emotions and more able to talk about our problems and get them out in the open. Men have a tendency to bottle it all up or ignore it until it's too late, until it builds and builds and becomes overpowering. I know we're supposed to be living in the age of the 'metro-sexual man', where blokes are more in tune with their feminine sides and happily use skincare products, but there's still a long way to go before you'll walk into a coffee shop of an afternoon and see a group of men sitting there sipping lattes and gossiping about their problems. I hate to say it, and I know it's a bit of a generalization, but most men are still emotionally repressed.

And this can lead to huge problems when they suddenly become faced with stress and anxiety. They can't cope and, if you don't have any way to offload your problems, they become such an issue that they take on a life of their own. This was what happened to Graham. I've spoken before about him. He was such a lovely young man, a friend of a friend of my daughter Fern. He was a soldier and got sent to serve in Afghanistan when he was twenty-two years old. When he finished his tour of duty, he made an appointment to come and see me. At that point, I had never met him but, because of the vague family connection, I found a spare hour in the diary.

He was a typical army boy. He arrived at my doorstep dot on time dressed in combat trousers, polished black boots and a tight white vest. He had intense eyes and short-cropped hair, and you could tell that he was a very fit young man.

We sat together in my office and I noticed how upright he was, straight-backed and almost standing to attention. I tried to relax him a bit with some chit-chat. It was obvious he was slightly apprehensive about being with me and I wondered briefly why he had made the appointment. He didn't seem the type of person who would come to see a medium. I do get young men coming to see me, particularly gay men. I have a huge gay following. Graham most definitely was not gay.

'Have you ever been to see a medium before?' I asked him. He told me that he hadn't, so I asked him why he had decided to come now.

You see, young people don't spend much time wondering about spirit and pondering the afterlife, so I assumed he wasn't with me out of curiosity.

'I want to know if there is an afterlife,' he replied.

I was surprised. It was such an unlikely thing for a young guy to say.

While he had been sitting there, I had opened myself up to spirit and I had a gentleman with me: Graham's grandfather.

I told Graham that there was indeed an afterlife and that I had his grandfather with me and his name was Bill. I gave him more detail that confirmed that Bill was indeed in the room with us, and Graham was impressed and seemed relieved in a way.

The reading continued, and Graham talked about a relationship he had been in which had failed and how unhappy he was about that. He also spoke about how one day he wanted to have children. The strange thing was that I didn't see kids in his future. He was quite tearful during the reading, and it was a powerful one. There was a lot of energy around him and there seemed to be a lot of other people in spirit who came to him.

All the way through I could tell he was troubled. I could see there was something weighing him down. It was only very near the end of our time together that he revealed what it was.

I had picked up from his energy that he was grappling with a big decision, and I told him that I felt there was something big that was due to happen to him in the following six weeks. He explained that he was going to be posted to Iraq and that he really didn't want to go.

Then he told me why. In Afghanistan, he had been part of a patrol that had been sent into a house where suspected Taleban fighters were hiding. He was with a small detachment of three others. One of them was his sadistic senior officer. They smashed their way through the door of this mud-walled building and, sure enough, there were four men inside.

He explained, 'The leader of our squad was a right bastard and wanted us to kill one man each. He slotted the first, and the other two guys I was with followed. But I couldn't kill. There was one guy left cowering in the corner. He was the youngest of the lot, younger than me, and he looked terrified. He was jabbering away, begging for his life, I suppose.'

Graham told the other men he couldn't do it, he couldn't kill an unarmed man. So they killed him instead.

As he was telling me this awful story, he broke down in pained sobs and said that was why he couldn't go to Iraq. He couldn't bear what he had seen and been asked to take part in. He couldn't buy himself out of the army and he couldn't complain about what had happened because you don't do things like that in the army. In war you all stick together.

I felt desperately sorry for him, but when I looked into his future I couldn't see Iraq. I told him so. I told him everything would be OK and that he didn't have to worry.

Before he left, he seemed to change. He straightened back up and he seemed OK, as if he had switched back into army mode.

'I just need to know that you have my granddad and that there is a Heaven,' he said.

'Of course there is,' I reassured him.

Three days later, he was dead. He had locked himself in a car in a garage, sealed the doors and windows and started up a chainsaw on the back seat. He was killed by carbon-monoxide poisoning.

When I heard, I was devastated. I couldn't understand why I had failed to see his death, and for a time the whole tragic episode made me doubt my ability, for the first time. In the end, though, I think what that reading proved to me was that I'm just not meant to see a person's death before it happens, no matter how immediately in the future it is. We all pass when our time has come, and there's not a thing I can do to alter that.

About a year after Graham died I was doing a show in Cornwall and, as I walked into the theatre, a woman approached me and said hello. She said she wanted to thank me and introduced herself as Graham's mum. I felt desperately sad for her and told her how terrible I'd felt when he died. She told me that she had found the tape recording of our reading that I had given to Graham. I make tapes for everyone I read for so they can go away and listen again, as often the messages only become apparent weeks, months or even years later.

His mum explained that just knowing that Graham had believed in the afterlife and that his grandfather would be there waiting for him had given them much comfort in the dark months after his death.

To this day, I feel sad that Graham felt unable to unburden himself and had decided that his only option was to end his life. He was suffering a deep mental anguish. That he'd taken the course of action he had was a tragedy, but it certainly wasn't a sin.

The Village of Lost Souls

Can a whole town be infected by suicidal energy? It sounds crazy, doesn't it, but it happens. There are many cases where suicide seems to spread through a town like an infection. You read about it in the newspapers. Suddenly, within the space of a few months, several people in the same area take their lives. Usually, they are youngsters – most often, teenagers – and, usually, they know each other.

From our vantage point on this side of the divide between life and death, it all seems like such a waste and so pointless, but step into the afterlife and our point of view is no longer relevant. All that matters is that the dead are at peace.

I experienced the spirit side of one of these suicide outbreaks, if you can call them that, when I held a show in Perth, Scotland, a few years ago.

It started with a hijacked message. I had picked up the brother of an elderly woman in the audience and, as I was talking to her, the image of a broken plank of wood slotted into my mind. Where did that come from? I thought to myself, and asked the woman, 'Was there a piece of timber or something that got smashed in half?'

She shook her head, bemused.

There was no doubt about what I was being shown – the image was strong and clear – so I persisted. Another spirit then came into focus: a teenage boy. And I knew that he had taken his own life. He had hanged himself. He appeared directly in front of me, in human form, and pulled me to the other side of the stage. I realized it was a completely different message to the one that I had been delivering. He had sabotaged the reading, and he was insistent. I told the lady that her brother was fine and at peace and had to move on to this new message. I'm sure she was disappointed that I couldn't give her more but, unfortunately, that is what happens with mass readings. There is no queuing system, like at the deli counter in the supermarket; I just pass on what I hear. There were over a thousand people in the audience and, if each of them has someone waiting for them in spirit, that's a prospective one thousand-plus messages. There's no way I can order all that information. I just have to go with the flow and let spirit direct me.

'I have a young boy here,' I told the audience. 'I know that he committed suicide. I see a plank of wood, and it's broken in the middle.'

I heard the name Daniel being whispered to me in my mind, and relayed it to the audience.

'I think he hanged himself,' I added.

Then another name: 'Graham?' I said.

A middle-aged lady in a purple top stood nervously.

'Graham was a close friend,' she told me. I didn't know it at the time, but Graham had died in 2004. He lived in a village called Auchtermuchty and, within the space of a few years, several young people had died in the same area. They had all taken their own lives.

I continued: 'So who is Daniel?'

A younger woman who was with Graham's friend

stood with her to explain. 'It was the name of his house,' she said. 'It was called Dan's.'

Suddenly I saw the relevance of the broken wood. There is nothing random about spirit, you see. I saw a bench in a graveyard, a memorial bench, and the plank across the middle of the seat had been broken.

I told the women, 'If you go to his bench, someone has jumped on it. It's broken.'

But once again, spirit had a trick up its sleeve.

'That's not Graham's bench, that's another of my friends. They're in the same cemetery,' explained the second woman. 'There were a few of them; they all killed themselves. One of the others had his bench vandalized the other day.'

I was given a date: the 17th. It was the date that the boy whose memorial bench had been vandalized had died: 17 March.

So I had two teenagers in the same cemetery who had both lived in the same village and had both taken their own lives. And, in the audience, I had two women who knew them. You can't tell me there's anything coincidental about that.

And it got even stranger.

A while later, I picked up the names Gordon, and what sounded like Kerrie and Kirana.

Immediately, a lady stood up.

'My daughter is Kiana, I'm Corrie and my brother was called Gordon.'

Gordon was only twenty-nine and had taken his own life a few years before.

He had a message.

'He says he isn't cold,' I related to the women. 'He says it's just his body that is cold and he's no longer in his body.'

I later learned the relevance of this information. Gordon's mum went to visit her son in the mortuary after he died. He looked so peaceful and she bent down to gently kiss his cheek. As she did so, she drew back in shock. His lifeless skin was so cold. She had always been troubled by this but had never spoken to anyone about it. It was a moment in her life that I captured.

Then came the psychic *coup de grâce*.

Another name popped into my head.

'Is there anyone called Anne Marie?' I asked Gordon's sister.

She turned and pointed to the two women I had been speaking to earlier whose friends had both committed suicide in Auchtermuchty. Marie Anne was the older woman's daughter. She was also in spirit and had also come from that fated village.

It was an amazing reading, one of the most mind-bending I can remember. All those spirits from that small village had swarmed in that night to let the world know they were safe and sound in Heaven.

Curiouser and Curiouser . . . Down the Psychic Rabbit Hole

I was having a natter with a friend of mine the other day. We were sitting in a coffee shop enjoying a cappuccino (since the gastric bypass I can only manage half a cup, which is a shame, because I do love a coffee), when she looked at me very seriously and said, 'How do you stay so upbeat, Sal?'

'What do you mean?' I frowned.

'Well, your work, it's all death, isn't it? That's what you do: you speak to dead people every day. Surely it gets depressing?'

But I don't really think about what I do that way. After all, I've been in contact with the dead since before I can remember, so to me they are just there: it's normal for them to be there.

She continued, 'I mean, you've seen some terrible, terrible things. You have to make contact with dead children and speak to bereaved mothers, you've picked up murder victims and people who have committed suicide. How can you do that day in and day out and not get ground down by it all?'

I suppose she was right. On one level, there's a lot of what most people would call doom and gloom associated with my work. After all, death and bereavement *are* sad. Losing loved ones is a sad part of life, and bereavement is the hardest thing most of us will ever experience. But I explained to her that the other side of my work is the hope and closure I can bring.

In a way, it's similar to doing a job like a paramedic or a surgeon: they see some very sad things too sometimes, but they get the opportunity to help people and to save them. I don't profess to do anything as fundamentally decisive as saving lives, and I'm no medical expert, but I do get to help people. Sometimes I'm in the privileged position of being able to give them immense comfort and help them turn their negative emotions into something positive. There are certain jobs where you have to experience some uncomfortable things in order to bring some benefit, and being a medium fits into this career bracket.

The trick is to concentrate on the positives and not to dwell on the negatives. And, anyway, it's often the case that, after an accurate reading, any negatives disappear, be they doubts or questions or fears.

So what on earth have I got to be sorry for? I get to do some amazing work, to meet some wonderful people and to make their lives a little better, even if it's only for the two hours they come and see my shows.

Then, while I was pondering this with my pal, I began to laugh. Because although the subject matter I deal in is death, it's not all sadness. Far from it. There's plenty of fun to be had in the afterlife! Sometimes things get so bizarre, I just have to laugh. And that laughter helps spirit. I've observed over the years that they love the energy laughter produces. I have another one of my theories that relates to laughter.

I think laughter makes the energy in a room easier for

spirit to navigate. If you think of energy as being like the weather, sometimes foggy, cloudy and heavy with turbulence and rain, other times still and clear with no pressure, I think that calm weather state is how spirit experiences energy when there is laughter and good humour in a room. We feel it too. That intuitive part of us that is so often closed can still feel a positive vibe in a room, can't it? Laughter is one way to create a vibe like this. In the case of a theatre show, laughter unifies an audience. When everyone is laughing at the same time, the energy is light and uniform; it vibrates in unison, and for spirit that means it is easier to move through.

I think it also helps that I am naturally an upbeat person. If I had a dial in my brain that ranged from 'ecstatic' to 'depressed', it would be permanently set on 'happy-as-Larry'. That's just the way I am, and I think spirits recognize this and tune into it because it makes it easier for their energy to link with mine. Think of it as spaceships docking: it only works if there are no obstructions. I also maintain a sense of wonderment at what I do, and that is invaluable too. I am forever amazed by some of the messages I get and some of the things I'm shown.

In fact, I don't think I could do this work if I didn't have a sense of humour, fascination and awe. I get the feeling it just wouldn't work and that the ability would switch itself off.

Never Work with Spirits or Animals . . . or Animals in Spirit

'I talk to dead people!' That's become my catchphrase over the last few years. I never meant it to, but I find myself saying it all the time, usually with a sense of incredulity, because sometimes I have trouble believing it myself. It's mad, isn't it? Me, little old Sally Morgan, can actually speak to the dead!

You'd think that, once I'd accepted my ability to contact the other side, nothing else would ever surprise me. Surely that is strange enough, right? But you'd be wrong. Nearly every day something will happen that is so mind-bogglingly bizarre and strange that I find myself laughing at the weirdness of it all.

Take the time I was joined by a seal. Yep, that's right: a great big blubbery seal. As far as my mind was telling me, it was standing there on stage next to me as clear as day. I could see its whiskers twitch and smell the fish on its breath.

You see, spirits like to have a laugh as much as we do. They get just as much of a kick out of raising a chuckle and playing a trick as we do on earth plane. When you pass over, you might lose the pain, the suffering and the negativity, but you don't lose your sense of humour or your sense of fun. So, this particular day, I found myself confronted by a big seal, sitting there resting on its flippers and looking at me with big, quizzical eyes. I stared back at it with raised eyebrows.

What the . . .? I thought, a smile playing on my lips.

I was giving a reading to a lady at a show, and all I could do was shrug.

Here we go, I said to myself.

The lady's name was Barbara, and I had her mother in spirit.

I sucked in a breath (of fishy air) and looked at her.

'Right,' I began, 'you know a seal? The animal?' I made a honking noise and started clapping my hands to mimic flippers (OK, I know I was doing a sea lion, but I'm no David Attenborough). 'Well,' I continued, 'there's one here next to me.'

I was assuming there would be someone connected with Barbara who worked in a zoo with seals. I expected Barbara to either laugh at me or circle her temple with her finger in a 'She's mad' gesture.

But Barbara didn't. She looked me straight in the eye, smiled and nodded her head.

'Yep, I know what you mean,' she said.

I was gobsmacked.

'You . . . you don't collect seals,' I stuttered.

'Yes, I love them.' She laughed.

I just stood there staring at her, my mouth wide open.

You know how some people come from horsey families, and some from dog or cat families? Well, Barbara came from a seal family. They all loved seals, and her mum had a toy seal in her bedroom which had huge sentimental value. But rather than show me a cute cuddly soft-toy seal, Barbara's mum had stuck a real seal next to me, just so her daughter knew she was there.

What are the chances of that? There standing next to

me was a floppy seal flapping its flippers together. I could have touched it and got my fingers wet it was that clear. I can totally understand the sceptics and the cynics who say, 'She is a cold reader or a guesser,' but where did that seal come from? A cat or a dog and you have half a chance. But a seal? It was the first time I had ever seen a psychic seal and I had to laugh.

'Your mum is fine, and your mum has given you a seal,' I giggled, indicating the space next to me.

Barbara didn't need any more confirmation. Her mum had come through and shown the most relevant but obscure thing she could to prove her presence.

'Is she leaving it for me?' Barbara asked.

'It's gone now.' I shrugged.

I don't get bothered by the bizarre things – they add to the readings – and although that seal was bizarre to me, it wasn't bizarre to Barbara.

By now of course I'm used to seeing people in spirit, but when I see animals it always surprises me for some reason, and it makes me smile. They still retain their playfulness, especially dogs. They can be disruptive in some cases and blunder in just like they do in life.

I was on stage once giving a reading to a girl in the audience. She had lost her friend – he had died of leukaemia – and she had spent hours with him in hospital as he underwent treatment which, sadly, proved ineffective. He had come through to say how grateful he was for her support and love, and to let her know that, although he was terribly ill and weak when he died, he no longer suffered and now watched over her from the afterlife. It was a poignant and emotional reading, as you can probably imagine.

And then I heard it. A *slap, slap, slap* noise. It was the noise of rubber on wood, and as I looked down to where the noise was coming from I saw a ball bounce across the stage. A second later a dog ran after it, from the left to the right of the stage. It was oblivious to anything else other than the ball. I gave a little gasp and stepped back. For a second I couldn't register whether it was a real dog or a dog in spirit. But what would a real dog be doing running across the stage of a psychic show?

I continued with the reading.

'His gran came for him,' I told the young girl. 'She held his hand and stroked his face at the end. It was very peaceful and he wasn't suffering any more. All the pain had gone.'

She sniffed, wiped her eyes and smiled at my reassuring words.

Then I heard it again. *Slap, slap, slap.*

The ball bounced past me once more. To my left I heard panting and the patter of little claws on the wood of the stage. The dog materialized again. It was a small wire-haired terrier with a scruffy tan coat and grey-flecked dark hair hanging like a beard around its muzzle.

It skittered past me and then stopped, turned and trotted back, looking up at me. I stared down at it in silence. The audience must have wondered what on earth was going on. Then the cheeky little scamp grabbed the hem of my long coat in its mouth and gave it a tug. Then it trotted off.

As the dog yanked my clothes I shrieked and, when I did, so did a woman in the front row of the audience.

I looked at her in amazement.

'You didn't just see what I saw, did you?' I asked.

'Something just pulled your coat,' she said. Although she hadn't seen the dog, she had seen my clothes move.

It didn't register with anyone else, just this one woman standing in front of me. Why had she seen my clothes move when no else could? Well, remember my valve theory and my belief that psychic ability is the heightened state of our natural intuitiveness? I reckon this woman's valve was a bit more open than those of the rest of the audience, and because of that she was a bit psychic. I often get psychics coming to my shows. They come to check out the competition. But this woman probably never even realized she had the ability to see things in spirit before that night. Thanks to that dog, she now knows.

Hanky Panky

Spirit animals are strange, but that old adage 'There's nowt so queer as folk' rings as true in death as it does in life. I get to see some strange things and look inside some weird minds when I'm open to spirit. Take Michael, for instance.

He came to see me several years ago, and I welcomed him into my office with a smile and a handshake. He'd been waiting outside in the front room chatting to John about football.

He was smartly dressed in a pinstriped grey business suit with a crisp white shirt and paisley-print tie. He must have been in his late fifties, but I could tell he liked to look after himself. As he sat down opposite me in my little office I caught a waft of expensive cologne – Acqua di Parma, I think it was, one of those lovely, timeless fragrances the old film stars used to splash on.

I'd never met Michael before but had seen his wife on many occasions. She was a lady who lunched. She didn't work and, thanks to a maid and the cleaner, she had plenty of time on her hands. You see, Michael was a very successful businessman. He worked in finance – something to do with hedge funds, whatever they are – and it made him a lot of money. Their two children had left home and Michael and his wife were knocking around a huge townhouse in Belgravia with plenty of time and money on their hands.

After his wife had raved about me, he had decided to book an appointment for a bit of business advice. I get a lot of businessmen coming to see me. It makes perfect sense. If you can read the markets, if you can make accurate predictions about the price of gold or wheat or whatever it is you deal in, you have an advantage over your competitors. I used to consult regularly for a businessman in Hong Kong who would call almost daily for predictions. I must have been right most of the time because he was a multi-millionaire.

Michael had never been to see a psychic before and, although he was polite, I sensed that he was sceptical. It happens all the time and I don't have a problem with it. I would expect people to be sceptical – after all, the claims I make are pretty fantastical.

So as Michael made himself comfortable I explained a little bit about what I did.

'I open myself to spirit and communicate with them. I'll answer any questions you have and be guided by whatever it is you want from this reading. I can look into aspects of your life and advise you on them, if that's what you want me to do,' I said.

Michael shifted in his seat. I detected a nervous energy coming from him.

'What, you can read my mind?' he said, slightly mockingly.

'I can see things about you, yes.'

He laughed.

When I give a reading, I don't just see spirit, I can see into every facet of the receiver's life, and as I opened myself up I saw as plain as day why Michael was a little bit uncomfortable.

An image swam into my mind. It was Michael. He was standing in a plush bedroom in front of a full-length antique mirror. He was standing in profile, shoulders back and head raised in a proud pose. He was admiring himself and I sensed a thrill of excitement coursing through him. To the side of the huge divan bed in the room there was an ornately carved wooden chest of drawers. One of the drawers was open and clothes had spilled from it as if they had been pulled out in a frenzy. Some were scattered on the floor, some on the bed. The garments were all expensive ladies' lingerie. And Michael was wearing some too. He had the full get-up on: sheer black stockings, suspender belt, French knickers and a silk camisole. Michael was a cross-dresser.

Then another flash. Michael arriving at work in his City office. It was early in the morning and, as he walked through the glass-fronted lobby of the building, he said hello to the cleaner, who was just finishing mopping the marble floor. Michael was carrying a briefcase and he was heading furtively for the toilets, taking it with him. He checked the cubicles first and when he was satisfied the room was empty he ducked into one, locked the door and pulled out a pair of hold-up black stockings. He removed his shoes, socks and trousers and put the stockings on, pulling them up over his briefs.

Michael definitely had a few issues.

As a rule, men are more reserved when they come to me. They don't open up like women do; they wait for me to tell them what I'm seeing. Michael certainly wasn't going to tell me that he loved to wear stockings and suspenders. Maybe he thought I wasn't a real medium, maybe he wanted to test me – or, possibly, he wanted me to find out. Sometimes being found out by a stranger helps people come to terms with their secrets and scruples.

I don't judge. I'm very open-minded, and when it comes to people like Michael and their habits, I try to empathize and understand. I've seen it all, believe me. It takes a lot to shock me and, whatever his motivations, I knew Michael wanted to share his secret with me.

I cleared my throat and leant forward.

'I know about your secret, Michael,' I said.

I didn't have to say any more. He burst out crying.

'I want to tell my wife,' he said.

He had desperately wanted to reveal his secret to his wife for years, but it had become such a hidden part of his life, buried and covered over, that he didn't know how to broach the subject.

I gave him the best advice I could. I advised that it would be best to tell her first, not to show her. I didn't need spirit to tell me that, it was common sense.

'If you just blunder in, drop your trousers and stand there in your shirt, stockings and suspenders, it may be a bit too much for her,' I said. After all, I would think it was a joke if John did that to me.

'You must think I'm a weirdo,' he said sadly, looking for reassurance.

'Who am I to say what's right or wrong.' I shrugged. 'All I know is that keeping this secret is making you sad. But if doing it makes your head normal and if it makes you feel balanced, then what's the harm? We all have quirks; every one of us has something we'd be embarrassed about if someone else knew.'

Michael drew comfort from that, and I hope he felt a weight lifted. The rest of the reading was about his business and his family life, and I don't know what he did when he left, whether he told his wife or not. I just hope I helped him in some way.

Hang-ups and foibles like Michael's are the little glitches in our personalities that make us what we are. Michael saw me in the privacy of my own home, but imagine what it must be like to have your secrets told to an audience. Well, it does happen. Spirits sometimes come through with the most bizarre messages.

One such reading that always makes me laugh when I think back on it happened at a show a while back. An elderly woman came through and was calling for her daughter, Tracey.

Remember I explained that spirits often show me facets of their former characters to allow people to identify them? Well, this lady came through, and I got the impression she had liked a drink when she was alive. I was swaying a bit as her energy ran through me.

An attractive slim lady in the audience stood up to take the message. She was reluctant at first, and I found out why a few minutes into the reading!

The spirit first showed me scissors and hair being cut, and the lady in the audience confirmed that her mother used to be a hairdresser.

'Who is Molly?' I asked as a name materialized in my head.

'Molly is my daughter,' she said.

Then things got weird. In my mind I heard a slapping sound, like skin being smacked. I made a slapping motion with my hand and through the noise I heard a name.

'Who's Barry?'

The lady looked confused.

The old lady in spirit was showing me the image of a man and in the image he was with the lady in the audience. She was leading him into her house.

'Do you let someone called Barry into your house?' I asked.

'Not Barry, Gary,' she said. And then she started giggling uncontrollably. She hid her face in her hands.

Then the lady in spirit showed me another scene. In the interests of decency, I won't go into the finer details of what I was seeing here, but I will say it involved spanking.

'He doesn't spank you, does he?' I asked as the audience erupted in laughter. The woman in the audience shook her head and went as red as a beetroot.

'She's seen that,' I told her. 'Each to their own, that's what I say. We're all adults here. But just remember, your mother is watching.'

The lady took it all in good humour. What could I do? I could only tell her what I was being shown.

I do think that spirits can watch people making love, kissing, being naughty and sexy. It's a sobering thought, I know, but there you go: they like to be around us.

Sometimes they even keep their earthly desires with them when they cross over. Because the love we have is the thing we take with us, if we have a loving relationship that is particularly passionate, that passion remains.

Take Fred, for example. He came through at a show in Dorking, Surrey. It was a busy night, the energy was strong and clear and Fred came through as sharp as a pin. His daughters and his wife were in the audience and, to begin with, one of his daughters stood to take the message. Fred tenderly thanked her for nursing him when he was ill. It was an incredibly moving exchange. And then Fred picked up on the energy of his wife. And that really got him going!

He showed me details of their relationship that made me blush.

'He used to run his hands up your arm,' I said, papering over the more raunchy images Fred was showing me.

His wife, an elderly lady with a sparkle in her eye, laughed.

'He still wants to touch you,' I said. I could feel Fred's energy pulsing, eager to make the connection to his wife.

'He always did,' she laughed.

'Being close to you keeps his energy up,' I said.

'He was always very energetic,' she agreed.

Spirits also often show me the places they return to in order to be with their loved ones. They're usually the places that meant most to them in life, the sentimental places where they shared meaningful times with their loved ones, such as favourite beaches or family homes. Fred told me exactly where he'd be waiting to make a connection with his wife.

'When you're in bed, you'll feel something running up your arm. That'll be his hand,' I told her. I felt like a psychic Cilla Black: I'd just fixed up a date between dead Fred and his living wife!

Love and laughter so often go hand in hand in life, and the same applies in death. Some of the most touching and outwardly tragic readings and messages I have had the honour of giving are often punctuated by laughter. The humour is usually instigated by spirit. It's spirit's way of easing the pain of those left behind. After all, they aren't sad, they're happy and content in the afterlife, so they don't want us to be miserable about their passing.

I read once for a woman who had lost her lover two months before they were due to fly abroad to Mexico to get married. He died suddenly, and the poor woman had found him dead in bed. She still went ahead on the holiday they had booked and he came through to let her know that, on the date they were due to be married, he was there with her. He described himself as her permanent partner, which made her laugh, because they never got the chance to get hitched. He wanted her to know that he loved her very much and also, like Fred, he wanted her to know that she would feel him in bed. To demonstrate this he showed me images of their relationship, much as Fred had. Really personal ones!

'Too much information,' I laughed.

I don't know who was more embarrassed, me or his partner. I'm sure spirit doesn't reveal those kinds of memories to me on purpose. I think, in the heat of the moment, they just slip out by accident. It's lucky I'm so broad-minded.

'He's a naughty boy, isn't he?' I told the lady, and moved swiftly on.

It's All Greek to Me

I've had it all in my career as a medium. I've had drunks and junkies, murderers and dead celebrities. I take it all in my stride, but I'm still capable of being baffled by what I hear and feel. Sometimes it's all Greek to me – literally, in one case, when the spirit of a lady came through and spoke in a language I couldn't understand.

It had never happened before but I suppose, given that thousands of people have come to my shows over the years, it was inevitable it would happen one day.

The words flashed into my mind, and I didn't have a clue what they meant or even how to pronounce them. I felt like a right Charlie standing there on stage trying to repeat what was going through my head. It didn't help that the lady in spirit who was feeding the words to me wasn't being particularly patient.

'Erm, someone is saying to me 'Broosha' or 'Breesha'?

The words were coming through in a thick, deep accent.

The audience looked at me blankly until a lone hand went up a few rows from the front. A dark, long-haired, swarthy middle-aged man stood up.

'Hello,' he said in the same thick, treacly accent I was hearing in my head.

'Oh, hello,' I said, raising my eyebrows. 'What have I said that makes sense?'

He told me that the word 'brush-tie' (I'll write it as it

sounds because I haven't clue how it's spelt) means 'in the front' in Greek – where he was sitting: in the front of the stalls.

'Get out of it!' I squealed. 'The message is for you.'

Then I got another word: 'Coula.'

'That is a Greek name,' he explained. 'It is my great-aunt's name.'

As I was talking to him, a sound kept interrupting my thoughts. *Sh-sh-sh-sh-sh.*

I explained what I was hearing to the audience.

'It is not like a *shush* sound,' I said. 'It's like a constant *sh-sh-sh-sh* sound.'

Whatever strange noise I was hearing registered immediately with the man who had taken the message.

'Ah yes, she has done that before,' he smiled.

I was confused.

Then he explained.

'She means, "Be quiet. 'Don't talk."' He laughed.

Apparently, in Greek, rather than saying 'Shush!' to someone, you quietly say 'Shshshsh'. I was being told to shut up by the spirit of this man's great-aunt!

So I've had seals, playful dogs, bilingual readings . . . I've had the lot. My theory is that by doing shows for so many people the psychic energy builds up so intensely that it opens the way for all kinds of psychic messages and phenomena to come through. And people are much more open to it because they're in a crowd. They feel the energy in the room, and that collective energy of a show helps to open everyone's valve a few more notches.

Another result I've found from this increased energy build-up is that I see orbs at my shows. I believe orbs happen when a spirit's energy is so strong it begins to glow like an electrical charge. I'm convinced that, sometimes, the energy levels get so high, spirits actually fizz. They can be seen, like tiny shooting stars.

The most amazing orb showed itself at a theatre in Buxton. I was on stage, facing the audience. My cameraman was zooming in on me and so my image was on the screen behind me as I addressed the auditorium. I was giving a particularly tense reading to a woman further back in the stalls. Suddenly there were screams breaking out from all over the auditorium. Some of the people in the front row were pointing to the screen behind me. I didn't have a clue what was going on and spun round to see what they were looking at. And there, on the screen, I saw a bright orb hovering above my head. And as the audience and I watched open-mouthed, the orb left my head and drifted slowly but directly across the room and stopped above the head of the woman who was receiving the reading. It hung there, motionless. The whole theatre saw it.

If any sceptics had came to see me that night, I have a funny feeling their doubts would have disappeared after that spectacle.

Jeff and Jade

'Jeff who?' I asked.

I was sitting in a hotel room surrounded by cameras and lighting equipment and there was a man waiting outside. I was due to give him a reading and I hadn't a clue who he was. Apparently, according to one of the producers, he was a TV presenter.

We were filming the celebrity segments of my first TV series, *Sally Morgan: Star Psychic*. I'd seen plenty of famous people and celebrities in the past, in the days before I was lucky enough to have my own television show, but I wasn't a great follower of celebrity news. I was too busy to get involved in all that. I didn't know my Kerry Katonas from my Susan Boyles and I didn't rush off down the newsagents each week to get my fix of *Heat* magazine.

So when they mentioned the name Jeff Brazier to me I didn't know who they were talking about. It was only when they mentioned he was Jade Goody's former partner that I had a vague recollection. I knew Jade; everyone knew Jade.

In those early days, it took a while for me to get my head around reading for celebrity clientele on camera. Working from home doing face-to-face readings for private clients was simple. They called, we booked them in, they came, they left. That was it. But with celebrities it was more a case of my production people speaking to their managers, and then there would be this odd kind of mating ritual where emails and calls would be exchanged and egos massaged before there was finally a contract. It was all over-complicated, as far as I could see.

But none of that mattered when Jeff bounced into the room, because the room lit up. His boyish face was fixed in a cheeky grin and his Essex accent was infectiously upbeat. Waves of positive and open energy radiated from him and, thanks to his sense of humour, which was always in the 'on' position, I could tell straight away that spirit would be attracted to him.

He gave me a big hug and we sat down for our reading. It was the beginning of a relationship that has lasted several years.

Before that first reading, as I say, I knew nothing about Jeff. On *Star Psychic* I was only told who I was due to be seeing minutes before I met them, either in the car on the way to the reading or just before the reading itself. And that's how I wanted it. I didn't want to open myself up to allegations that I researched the people I read for. I never did and I never have. With me given no warning, the readings were as authentic for the celebrities as they always had been for my other clients. I use spirit to guide me, not Google. That's the way it's always been with me and that's the way it always will be.

Anyway, in that first reading with Jeff, I didn't have an inkling of who he was or what he did, and I knew nothing about his family or his personal circumstance except that he once went out with Jade Goody.

As we sat in the room making idle chit-chat while the camera crew sorted out the technical stuff, I felt a presence in spirit anxious to come through. With it I felt deep sadness and unresolved issues.

This is going to be interesting, I thought to myself. And as we settled into the reading, I became aware that the presence that had materialized was Jeff's father. I could tell that he had only been young when he'd died.

As I explained to Jeff what I was seeing and feeling and what he could expect from the reading, I was shown his father's death. It was unique and tragic.

First I felt weightless, and I could sense panic all around me. In my mind's eye I was taken to a specific place and time. It was dark and cold and everything seemed to be moving in slow motion. I could see scenes around me lit up at intervals by a flickering light, as if a strobe light was flashing intermittently. In the semi-dark and icy cold, there was a feeling of fear and, in the background, there was a sound: *whomp, whomp, whomp*.

Then it clicked: Jeff's dad was underwater, but he was in a confined space. Sometimes, psychic scenes come to me in a vivid flash; other times, they build up gradually, with the detail uncovering itself like a picture being coloured in. I think the way these visual messages reveal themselves to me depends on the strength of the energy the spirit is endowed with and the detail of the scene I'm being shown. This scene revealed itself to me gradually and, as it unfolded in my mind, I saw the dark outline of a girl take shape in the distance. She was floating in the water and she wore a white dress. She was sinking, away from Jeff's dad. Her dress fanned out in the water and flowed around her like the fins of some exotic ghostly fish. Jeff's father was reaching out to her and in the flickering light I could see her eyes. They were dead. Her mouth was fixed open, her limbs were lifeless, suspended by the weightlessness of the water. She became smaller and more distant as she drifted away.

I related what I was seeing to Jeff, and he sat, with knit-ted brow, nodding at my description. Suddenly the jovial reading had turned very serious. I told him I believed his father had drowned.

Jeff then explained the relevance of my visions. He told me that his estranged father was a man called Stephen Faldo. He was a pleasure-cruise captain who piloted tour-ist boats up and down the River Thames. In the early hours of 20 August 1989, he was in charge of a boat on the river that was hosting a birthday party and was full of young people. They set off from a pier near the West End for a night of dancing and fun. There were 131 people on board. The boat was called the *Marchioness*. Just before 2 a.m., a huge dredger called the *Bowbelle* rammed into Stephen's boat, dragging it under the murky Thames and crushing it like a toy. Fifty-one people died in what became one of the biggest boating tragedies in London's history.

Jeff was amazed at my description, and after that first meeting we met again, not for the cameras but because he was interested in my work. I gave him readings, and he was always open-minded, though he remained sceptical at times as well.

I've said before that I don't think I'm supposed to see people's deaths. That isn't part of the plan. I don't look into the future of the people I read for and see them keel over on a certain day with a heart attack. Sometimes I get indications of health problems they have had in the past or may have in the future, but when it comes to the biggie, the expiration date, I believe that it is always meant to be a secret between the individual person and their maker. The same rules apply when it comes to the deaths of people connected to those I read for. I'm no more able to tell them when their Aunt Maude will pop her clogs than I'm able to tell them when they will.

It was because of this that I didn't pick up on the fact that, years after that first reading with Jeff, his life would be touched by tragedy once again. I wasn't shown what would happen to Jade.

Jeff came to see me again after she had been diagnosed with the cervical cancer that eventually killed her. The content of that reading must remain confidential. It's a matter between Jeff and spirit. At the time, Jade was adamant she would beat the disease, and Jeff was hopeful too. Again, I didn't pick up any indication that Jade would die when I focused on that part of his life and, given the circumstances of her illness and the stage it had got to, there appears there was little anyone could have done to save her.

Although Jeff was no longer with her when he came to see me (they had been apart for many years), the initial ill feeling between them after their split had mellowed with the years and they were good friends and devoted parents to their children. As Jade fought the illness, Jeff was a huge support to the mother of his two sons, Freddy and Bobby. As it became sadly apparent that she was losing her fight for survival, they worked out the heartbreaking details of how their sons would be raised without their mother.

Jade died on Mother's Day in March 2009 and, over a year later, Jeff came to see me again, this time for a reading as part of my *On the Road* show. Jeff and I have always got on well. He's a lovely boy with a wise head on his shoulders, and he's a brilliant dad. He makes sure the boys are protected from the glare of publicity and has provided a loving and stable home for them since their mother was so cruelly taken from them. As soon as Jeff sat down with me and I opened myself up to spirit, there was Jade, loud and clear, radiating a deep love for her sons.

The first thing I felt was her concern for her boys. She was showing me certain details about their health and, although she knew Jeff was taking good care of them, she wanted to highlight the particular concerns she had.

'I sense headaches around you,' I told him, as I felt a sharp stabbing pain in the middle of my forehead. Jade was allowing me to feel the pain that her eldest, Bobby, sometimes suffered.

'I get a terrific pain in my forehead. The person this relates to may have to get their eyes checked for vision problems, or it may be something they suffer from when they get overloaded – a sign that they need some time out,' I explained.

Jeff confirmed that Bobby got headaches when he was upset.

Then Jade turned her attention to Freddy.

'I'm looking at Freddy, and someone here is telling me about his hearing. That needs checking,' I continued. Bless her, Jade was giving Jeff a checklist from the afterlife. It was as if she was giving her boys the once-over and, like an over-protective mum, reminding Jeff to keep an eye on them, which he was doing very well.

Jeff confirmed that, after his mother's death, Freddy had had a few problems at school and one possibility that was investigated was his hearing. He was fine now but it had been a concern at the time.

As I saw the boys in my mind's eye, I also got the distinct feeling that Freddy's psychic *valve* was very open; that he was 'knowing', as I explained to Jeff. I was loathe to say 'psychic', because that term can be so loaded when it's given to a child. Suddenly everyone thinks you're like the kid in *The Sixth Sense*! But I certainly got the feeling that Freddy was sensitive and intuitive.

Jeff nodded.

'It wouldn't surprise me,' he said. 'Freddy is very different.'

Then Jade showed me something which, on the face of it, was horrific but which she thought was hilarious.

I was shown a scene. Someone was bent double in agony; it was a woman, but I couldn't see who because her hands were covering her face and blood was leaking through her fingers.

'Who had something go through their right eye?' I asked.

Jeff nodded. He explained: 'Jade managed to stab herself in the eye with some scissors, which is really hard to do. Only someone as special as Jade could have mastered that! I remember getting a call, she was in floods of tears, and I remember rushing home and taking her to Moorfield Eye Hospital in London, where they pulled them out for her. It's funny thinking about it now, but it was horrific at the time.'

With the benefit of hindsight, Jade thought it was hilarious too. Jeff was right – who else but Jade could have had such a bizarre accident?

The love and warmth I felt as Jade channelled her energy through me was immense. I could feel what a huge connection she had with her boys. She has been and will always be watching them. Before she died I remember reading an interview with her in which she revealed that she had told her family that, whenever they missed her, they should look into the sky. She explained to them that she would be the brightest star they could see. She promised her sons that, even though she had to leave them, she would always be watching over them from Heaven.

As I sat with Jeff, feeling the spirit of Jade practically glowing with deep maternal love, I knew she was keeping her promise.

There's a New Star in Heaven Tonight

Like Jade, some people are maybe just too full of personality and too full of energy to live on into old age, to grow old, wither and die. You know the type, the larger-than-life characters with personalities so big they create their own gravitational field of friendliness that sucks in everyone around them, people who are always surrounded by friends and laughter, the ones you know you'll always have a good time with.

Stephen Gately was one of these. He was a huge-hearted man with a zest for life so strong you could almost touch it. And I am proud to say he was a dear friend.

I enjoyed many a night of fun with Stephen and his partner, Andrew.

I'm not really a big drinker. I'm not one of these people who needs a couple of glasses of wine before they can relax and enjoy themselves. I can have a good time without the aid of artificial stimulants. If I have one weakness, however, it's champagne. I do like the odd glass of bubbly, and it was that weakness that left me standing in a restaurant in north London singing 'Hey Jude' with Stephen and my other showbiz buddy Natalie Imbruglia.

In life, there are always a handful of nights that stand out as the best times of your life. That night was definitely in my top ten.

We'd had a lovely meal in a restaurant called San Carlos,

and in the early hours of the morning the door was locked and there were just a few guests left. Stephen, who was always the life and soul of the party, decided to start a sing-along.

'Do you know "No Matter What"?' he asked the bemused restaurant pianist.

Sure enough, the guy did, and Stephen gave a note-perfect rendition of the Boyzone hit.

Well, that was like throwing down the gauntlet for Nat, who knows a thing or two about hit records herself.

Not to be outdone, she stood up as the guests cheered the end of Stephen's song and asked the pianist if he knew the tune to her hit 'Torn'. Again, he obliged, and she belted out the number. By now the place was rocking and I'd started to do readings for some of the customers. It must have been an amazing night to be there: a lock-in, two pop-star performances and a psychic reading! I was really getting in the swing of things and, when John egged me on to join Nat and Stephen, I didn't need to be asked twice. I jumped up and joined them, and the three of us sang the Beatles classic . . . well, they sang it, I just murdered it!

I had a tipsy grin on my face as wide a Cheshire cat's as I swayed back and forth with my arms around Nat and Stephen's shoulders singing the chorus. It's my favourite memory of Stephen. He was standing at the front of the restaurant, arms outstretched, with a big smile on his face encouraging everyone to join in. Music was his life, and he was such a talented individual.

I first met him several years ago when he appeared as a guest on *Star Psychic*. We instantly gelled. You couldn't help but like Stephen. Despite his boyish good looks, he'd been through the mill and out the other end, and life had definitely knocked a few corners off him, but he was a little angel really. Thanks to my ability, I'm a pretty good judge of character, and I could tell straight away that Stephen was one in a million, a real diamond, and despite his success he was always down to earth and genuine.

When we met, it was like fate bringing us together. I just fell in love with him. When I say I fell in love with him, it was like looking at a son. I felt quite maternal and protective towards him, and I think that's what he liked about me. He could be himself with me and he knew I wasn't judgemental.

Stephen had a big family in Ireland, but his work took him all over the world and most of the time he was based in London. I suppose I became like a mum or an aunty figure to him. He became a good friend of the family and was particularly close to Fern, my daughter. He'd come to family dos, and me and John would hook up with him and Andrew – just the four of us.

In the first reading I gave to him I saw lots of exciting projects in his future. I saw that he would have become a bestselling writer if fate had not intervened. And although he had solo success, when he saw how well Take That were doing after they re-formed, he was anxious to get Boyzone back together as well.

When the band did eventually re-form and started touring again, he was over the moon. He loved performing, he loved being on stage. He loved singing; it was what he was put on the earth to do.

We used to meet up and have dinner at The Ivy in the West End. Whenever we met we'd have pink champagne.

Stephen loved a glass of champagne, but essentially he was clean-living.

When he died, I hadn't seen him for six months. I'd been touring and, after the Boyzone project, he'd been madly busy too.

The strange thing was that, a few weeks before his death, I had a funny feeling that a celebrity was going to die. As I've mentioned, I don't see people's deaths when I read for them and I don't see the deaths of people close to them, but I do get premonitions, and about two weeks before Stephen died I was filming a reading for another celebrity when I suddenly screamed because I felt someone famous was going to die. At the time, I had the feeling it was going to be a woman, but after Stephen died I wondered if that premonition was a warning about his fate. I guess I'll never know.

The sad irony is that I heard about Stephen's death in the same way I heard about the death of another former client of mine, Princess Diana: I saw it reported on the television.

I'll never forget it. It was a Sunday morning, and John was downstairs watching television while I was upstairs getting ready. I love my Sunday lie-ins. It is one of the only days in the week when we don't book in shows, so it's become a bit of a ritual: lazing around, getting up late, having a family meal.

But this particular morning John called up urgently to me: 'I think you need to come down and see this.' I knew instantly by the tone of his voice that there was something wrong.

As I walked into the lounge, I flicked a glance at the television and the first thing that caught my eye was Stephen's name written in graphics on a headline. It read 'Singer Stephen Gately found dead in Majorca'. I gasped and looked at John. He was ashen, sitting on the settee staring at the screen and shaking his head.

After a few moments, the reality hit me as the newscaster detailed the circumstances in which Stephen had been found. The last time I'd heard from him was only two weeks before. He knew I was on tour and had asked to come to a gig. At that time, I had one of my flashes of 'knowing' that I often get when I speak to people and allow myself to open, and I felt he was starting a new journey.

As I watched the screen, I started crying. I grabbed my phone and frantically tried calling Andrew. I don't even know what I wanted to say, I just wanted to connect with him, and I held this vague hope that it was all some huge mistake. I must have left him I don't know how many messages.

As the reports unfolded, the implication was that there was something seedy about Stephen's death. Not only did his poor family have to cope with their loss, they also had to hear wild speculation about a possible link with drink, drugs, murder or suicide. There were all kinds of unfounded rumours and whisperings in the weeks after he died. In the end, tests proved that he had an undiagnosed heart problem and had died of natural causes. I knew Stephen well and was so upset to hear all the rumours. He was too upbeat to need to lose himself in drink and drugs.

To my deep regret, I didn't get to go to either his funeral or the memorial service held for him. I was working on both occasions and desperately tried to get back for the service but was held up. I feel bad about that, but I know Stephen would understand. After all, he was an entertainer too.

I still miss him desperately and often think about him. I've kept all the text messages he sent me; they're still on my phone. Sometimes when I think of him I read them and I feel a connection, although I would never make contact with him in spirit. It's not my place to barge in and do that. I know he's there in the afterlife, in Heaven, looking down on us all, but he needs to be invited in by his loved ones, by his family. That said, if Andrew wanted to contact him and asked me to facilitate it, I would happily oblige, but until then it isn't my place to meddle. If it does happen, though, I know Stephen will be there in spirit, standing next to Andrew with that trademark grin on his face.

That's Showbiz

It's ironic really. I now have my own television shows and sell-out tours and I get stopped and asked for autographs, but the whole 'Celebrity Psychic' label happened by accident. I never went out looking for fame and I certainly never went touting around for celebrity clientele. It's not as if I stood outside the Groucho Club or China Whites handing out my business card.

My association with stars happened gradually and without a plan. It happened by word of mouth really.

I suppose it all started with the Princess. She was the biggie and the one I'm known for. But even that happened by accident.

I had a friend who knew someone at Kensington Palace, the Princess's residence, and through her I was asked along to do readings for some of the staff there. Of course I jumped at the chance, and a few weeks after it was mentioned I found myself being ushered through the security gates just off Kensington High Street, up a driveway to the palace that might as well have been a different planet compared to the kind of places where I grew up.

With its manicured grounds, well-groomed staff, antique furniture and artwork, the property oozed breeding and class. I watched the staff as they performed their duties; they looked almost like robots, following the strict protocol that had been handed down through the ages. But away from their jobs they were just normal people with the same worries and concerns as all of us. I remember thinking that to have a career in that kind of environment you'd need to be a good actor.

I spent an afternoon sitting with several people who worked at the palace, reading for them and marvelling at the history and the energy of the building. What I didn't know was that, at the time, Princess Diana was sitting in the next room listening to me. She had always had a fascination with the spirit world and she couldn't help a sneaky listen to what her staff were getting up to.

She must have liked what she heard because I subsequently learned that she quizzed them on my abilities and even listened to the tapes some had made of their readings. She liked what she heard so much she wanted a go herself.

A few days after my excursion to the palace, I received a call from a senior member of the royal household, who would become my Diana go-between. She explained that the Princess wanted me to give her a reading but, rather than meet me face to face, she wanted to send me some items of sentimental value and see what I could pick up from them. I suppose this was Diana's way of testing me. She wanted to make sure I wasn't a charlatan and also that I could be trusted.

Some of the measures I later had to take when reading for her may have seemed paranoid at the time – things like decoy cars and sneaking through private entrances to her living quarters – however, it soon became obvious that Diana played a lifelong game of cat and mouse with the press and paparazzi and, in the incredible glare of publicity in which she found herself, some of those measures were necessary for her to have just a tiny semblance of normality in her life.

I was of course intrigued by all this cloak-and-dagger stuff and agreed to look at the things she sent. At the time I wondered why she didn't just invite me back to the palace but, as I learned later, the Princess often had her own unique way of doing things.

The following day my go-between arrived with a folded silk pouch. She sat in my office and unrolled it to reveal a watch and a pair of socks. The watch was beautiful, solid gold and so heavy it would have weighed your arm down. On the back it was engraved with the three-feather crest of the Prince of Wales and the date of his marriage to Diana. The socks were a pair of plain white gym socks – I know what you're thinking and, yes, they were clean!

The woman who had brought them gave me a piece of A4 paper filled with questions from the Princess. They were all handwritten. Using the watch and socks to tap into the psychic energy that linked to Diana, I answered all her questions and more. I taped the session and sent the tape back with the go-between.

Within two hours the phone rang.

'Mrs Morgan, this is the switchboard at Kensington Palace. I have the Princess of Wales for you.'

I couldn't even speak, I just grunted, and sat down in case my legs gave way. There was a click on the line and the next voice I heard was the unmistakable soft tones of Diana.

'Hello, Sally,' she said. 'Your tape was very interesting.'

The rest, as they say, is history. I was the Princess's personal psychic for several years. I've written at length about my dealings with her in my biography so I won't go into detail again here, suffice only to say that Diana was a fascinating person; she was funny, tragic and complex in equal measure. She had a great sense of humour and impeccable manners, and she never ever wanted to intrude on my life, as some clients did. In certain areas of her life she was deeply troubled and she just wanted to work out the best way forward for herself in the complicated life she led.

I stopped seeing her nine months before she died. My dealings with her ended as abruptly as they began. It wasn't because we fell out in any way, she just stopped contacting me. I know it was because, often, she didn't like what I was telling her. Sometimes people feel that familiarity breeds contempt, but that didn't happen with me and her. I certainly didn't get too familiar but, as with all the people I do readings for, it's no good coming to see me unless you want exactly what I get in my head, and there were things I was getting that related to Diana's personal life that she didn't want to hear. Still, I value the contact I had with her and I hold a lot of affection for the Princess. I was deeply shocked by her death and continue to lament the waste of such a vivacious life.

Once news leaked out that Diana was a client of mine, the ball started rolling and, since then, I've had a succession of celebrity clients which, I guess, put me on the path I am on now. Because of that first reading with her staff at the palace I've had some amazing experiences and met some amazing people.

One of my personal highlights was reading for guests at George Michael's birthday party a few years ago. What a night that was! I read for George and his partner Kenny

Goss. They were both huge fun and fantastic hosts. Sorry to say that I can't and wouldn't go into detail about the personal reading I gave George, but I did warn him at the time about certain habits which went on to cause him motoring problems in recent times.

Thanks to my shows, I've read for scores of celebrities. Some of them come back again and again. The first time I met *Coronation Street* star Kym Marsh she was so blown away she brought her mum in for a reading too, and I've read for her since. She's even been to one of my live shows. And ex-Atomic Kitten star Liz McClarnon is also a regular now.

Sometimes, though, the best ones are the cynics. I love to see their faces when I get one of those hits they just know has to come from somewhere inexplicable.

I had one such experience with the comedian Dave Gorman several years ago. He was doing a show on horoscopes and predictions and, for a magazine article, came for a reading. He was a genuine, warm person, not like some comedians, who compensate for their day jobs by being overly dour. But he wasn't convinced I could do what I said I could. Nevertheless, I started the reading and, halfway through, an image of a hand popped into my head. It was missing a finger.

'Who in your family has the second finger missing on their right hand?' I asked.

He was gobsmacked.

'My grandfather,' he answered. 'How on earth did you know that?'

It was spirit, of course!

TV presenter and *Strictly Come Dancing* star Gethin Jones was another avowed cynic. He was lovely and friendly but when he came for a reading when I was filming *On the Road* he was determined to try to catch me out.

'You could have known that anyway,' he said when I got his mum's name. 'She's famous in Cardiff.' But then when I told him how he had harboured ambitions to be a pilot but his vision had let him down, he had to concede there was no way I could have known that detail. He walked away and, to his credit, did admit that he had been surprised.

Thanks to my celebrity links, I also got the opportunity to go ghostbusting at Katie Price's house. She was having a few problems in her home and wanted to see if I would go along and shed some light on what was happening. You've got to laugh – this could only happen to Katie – but she believed her sunbed was haunted!

Part of our meeting was filmed for her reality show, *What Katie Did Next*, and also for my weight-loss documentary. She had recently met her second husband, Alex Reid, and he had moved into the house she'd once shared with her first husband, Peter Andre, in Woldingham, Surrey. The huge mansion was a former nursing home for the elderly and, as Katie met me at the door – managing to look glamorous with her hair scraped up in a bun and wearing a grey tracksuit – she explained that strange things had begun to happen after she had had building work carried out at the property. She was having problems with electrical appliances, her sunbed would turn itself on for no apparent reason and she had had to send a huge TV, part of her home-cinema set-up, back to the shop because it would inexplicably turn itself off.

I immediately felt there were problems. I could feel the presence of a woman dressed in white who used to live in the side of the house that would have been the residential area of the nursing home. She'd been one of the residents and had held the property in some regard, so her energy had remained. But the building work had changed the structure of the house and I felt that had disturbed her. She didn't mean any harm and she loved that the house was full of the sound of children and full of activity and excitement. It was just that she needed to get used to the new configuration. She wanted Katie to know she was there and that she too was part of the property.

Katie was fascinated by my investigation and explained that she had always harboured an interest in spirit. Away from the cameras, I gave her a personal reading and also explained that I was about to have surgery myself. As she was no stranger to the surgeon's knife, I asked her whether she thought gastric operations were a good idea.

'If you've tried exercise, if you've tried diets and if it hasn't helped and if you are unhappy with yourself, then the service is out there,' she said. 'Look into what you're having done, research it, know your doctor, don't go for the cheapest option and, as long as you're healthy and your heart can cope, do it.'

Then she added with a shrug: 'And if something bad happens, you'll be asleep and won't wake up anyway, so don't worry about it.'

I had to laugh.

PART THREE
Death is Just the Beginning

People often ask me how I feel about my own death.

'Bet you're not worried about dying at all, are you, Sal?' they say.

Well, I am! Even though I know that after I die I will be reunited with my loved ones and go to a wonderful place, I still don't relish the thought that I might be in pain at the end. I can honestly say I don't like pain – who does? – and if the end of my life means pain, then I'm not going to welcome it, am I? However, the comfort I have that many people do not is that I know what will happen once I have taken my last breath. There will be people waiting for me that I haven't seen for ages who love me, so although I am worried about the process of dying, if that involves pain and illness, I'm not afraid of death itself and I'm not afraid of where I'm going. I know that it isn't the end; I know it's the beginning of another part of my life.

I think that, in our culture, death gets a bad reputation. In some cultures it's welcomed, but we fear it.

Do you know how the dictionary defines the word 'death'? 'The event of dying or departure from life, the absence of life, the time at which life ends: a final state'. What a grim load of old baloney!

If I got the chance to rewrite the dictionary I'd put this: 'Death: the start of the good bit'.

Because that's what it is. It isn't the end for the person

who dies, because after death they get to experience the afterlife in all its glory. It only feels like the end for us, left on earth. We suffer that terrible acute sense of loss when a loved one dies and we tell ourselves we'll never see them again. It's a natural process but, believe me, it's not the truth. We will see them again. We'll be reunited when we die. Death is basically temporary separation. I'm sure if they have dictionaries in the afterlife the definition of death in those would say something like: 'birth into paradise'.

I know all this because I feel a little of what dead people feel. I get a sense of their very essence, I feel their energy channel through me, and it feels wonderful. I guess the most apt way to describe it is 'heavenly'. And if that is what death feels like count me in!

I always get the impression that spirits are at deep peace. Although they come through and show me aspects of their former lives which can appear disturbing or confusing or even painful, these feelings and details are just projections. They can't speak in the way we recognize because they no longer reside in their bodies, so they speak to me and send their messages through thought patterns, mental images and feelings. Underneath it all, though, they are serene and happy, and that probably has a lot to do with where they are, in their own personal paradise.

You see, I believe that Heaven, where our soul resides, is unique to each individual. I think it's what we want it to be, and most of us would like to feel we are somewhere at peace surrounded by love. I'm forever telling the people I read for that Heaven is a very special place and that it is full of love. It's a special kind of love, a deep love, not the fluffy and emotional love you feel when you are a teenager. The closest thing to it we'll ever experience on earth is the love we have for our children. It is unconditional, and it's what binds the dead to us. It's what ensures that none of us dies alone. Even if there is no one here on earth, even if you die on your own in a ditch somewhere, there will be someone waiting for you in spirit. Every one of us will have someone next to them in spirit when they die, someone waiting to take their hand and guide them into paradise.

It is this knowledge that I try to impart to everyone I read for. Even people in the most desperate of circumstances can gain comfort from it. It's the most important part of my work and the one thing that motivates me more than anything else.

Some of my clients come to me when they feel they have no hope left and, if I can prove to them the existence of an afterlife and send them away with hope, I know I have done what I am meant to do. For instance, take the mother I once saw who had an eleven-year-old daughter who was terminally ill. She came to me with no hope of a way out of her despair. The doctors had done everything they could, but the poor girl had a cancer that was inoperable and she had been given only months to live. Her mum was inconsolable. She was being eaten away and haunted by the suffering her child was going through and by the knowledge that, no matter what she did, her daughter would soon die. That's the awful thing about terminal illness: you mourn before the sufferer is dead. The mother came to see me three or four times, and I was able to link to people she knew in spirit and give her validation that they would be there waiting for her daughter. I was able to tell her things given to me by spirit that proved there is an afterlife, and she took that away and gained strength from it.

As I was reading for her, I could sense the power of spirit. They could feel her pain and they wanted to help. Spirits know when we are about to pass, and they congregate around us and wait for us. Terminally ill people often report seeing and hearing things. They often say they see shadows in the corner of their eye or feel a presence when they are on their own. That's the welcoming party! Because as soon as you pass there will be someone there who will say, 'It's OK. I'm here to look after you.'

When we're faced with a death, we go through the whole gamut of emotions. One of the most common themes I have found with bereaved people is guilt – guilt that they weren't able to do anything to save their loved ones and guilt that they weren't there when they passed. I know only too well how that feels, because I felt it too when John's father passed.

He was dying and was in hospital slipping in and out of a coma. We knew he was near the end of his life on earth, and he was clinging on till the very end. Like most of us, he was hard-wired with a strong survival instinct, and some days we would visit and he would be conscious, other days he would be unconscious and deathly pale.

The last time we visited was on a weekend, and he had slipped back into a coma. The doctors said that he was stable but that he would not regain consciousness. As we walked into the room, he was lying still on the bed. His breath was shallow and rattled in his chest and his head was bent forward. He looked peaceful and very close to giving up the fight. It was as if his life was ebbing away.

There was a nurse in the room fussing with the machines that were monitoring his breathing and heart rate.

'It's no good talking to him, he won't hear you,' she said.

But I knew differently and I knelt down and held his hand.

'It's Sally,' I said gently. 'We are here, you are not alone.' Out of the corner of his eye, a tear appeared, and it rolled down his face. Apart from that, he was completely still.

We sat with him for several hours into the evening but had to leave to go to an appointment. We told him we'd be back. A few hours later, we were at home getting ready to go back to see him when the phone rang. I knew what the person on the other end of the line was going to say before I answered.

Their voice was gravely serious:

'You should come to the hospital as soon as you can.'

We reached the hospital and ran through the corridors to the ward as fast as we could. Instinctively, we needed to be there, to be with him at the end. But as we got to his room a nurse was walking out and drawing the curtain around his bed.

'I am so sorry,' she said. 'He's just gone.'

John was devastated, and no matter how much I reassured him that everything was OK, that his dad was in a better place, it still didn't calm the guilt we felt at not being there during his last moments. But I knew that he did not die alone. I knew that he would have been helped into the afterlife by friends and family who would have come to get him.

Dying people can hold on up to a point – you hear about people sitting with terminally ill loved ones and they get up to go to the loo or get a cup of tea and when they come back the person is dead. Some people think that happens because there is a thread linking loved ones together and, as soon as that thread is broken, the dying person can float away. Personally, though, I'm not sure that's the case.

I think John's dad made his decision to die several hours before, and he waited until we had left him to pass to spare us the trauma of having to be there. I think that when I bent down and spoke to him that single tear was the only communication he could make, and with it he was telling us, 'I've had enough of this. There are people waiting for me on the other side. I'm off.'

The worlds of the living and the dead are inextricably linked. They exist in tandem, like the layers of an onion, but the door between them only opens one way. You can only cross from the living to the dead but, in certain circumstances, you can see and feel through the divide. That's where I come in. Certain people – intuitive people – have an ability to connect with the energy of the dead through the dividing line that separates our world from theirs. And spirit can see clearly through it. To them, it's like a one-way mirror: we can't always see them but they can see us, and they are constantly trying to make themselves known and felt.

But if you're not lucky enough to possess that level of intuitiveness, how will you know when they're around you? Well, you look for the signs, because there's no doubt: they do give us signs.

These signs come in many forms: it can be an unusually friendly robin in the garden, a white feather blowing on the wind or a butterfly dancing in the flowers. Signs can come in the form of a song on the radio. How many times have you thought about someone and a song that reminds you of them starts to play? That is spirit acknowledging your thought. Sometimes the signs come in dreams and other times they are just the hint of a breeze when all around is still. Spirit uses all our senses to let us know they are there.

Sometimes we'll get a whiff of a perfume that brings back memories of someone who has passed, or we'll smell food that reminds us of meals they used to prepare. All these little links to people we have known are signs that have been sent to us. And we can reciprocate these signs by regularly thinking of the people we have lost. Because just the act of a thought sends out a message of love, and that love is made of energy which crosses the divide and connects us with our loved ones. As long as we think about them and cherish their memories, we are maintaining the link between worlds and keeping those we think we have lost anchored to us.

I can never allow myself to get blasé about the messages I receive. I know how amazing it is to be able to tune into spirit, how lucky I am to possess my ability and how privileged I am when a spirit chooses me to be a messenger.

To the casual observer, often the messages I'm allowed the opportunity to impart will seem insignificant and trivial. Why would a loved one make all that effort to defy what many believe is the natural order of things, to cross the divide between life and death, only to tell a relative or friend something innocuous like where to find that old bracelet they recently lost or to be careful when climbing the stairs? Sometimes the messages are pure observation: a spirit will tell someone they witnessed them doing something like bumping their head or brushing their teeth. It doesn't sound remarkable, and cynics will probably say, 'Well, we all brush our teeth – what's the point of a message like that?' But the point is that it isn't the content of the message but the message itself that's important. The messages tell us that we are not alone, that we have not lost our loved ones. Not everyone has something profound to say in life, and that is equally true after death. What is important is the contact, the act of communication, because that allows the spirits to show that the bond between them and us has not been broken. That communication is validation that death is not the end. And that message, no matter how small, is comforting. When spirits talk to loved ones through me, they're telling them that they're still there; they're reaching out to the people they love. Spirits feel our grief and, although they can no longer give us a comforting cuddle, they can instead give us comfort just by saying, 'I am here with you.' So those messages that might seem inconsequential are actually vital to the people they are meant for. They are little pockets of hope, sent at a time when hope can seem to be in short supply.

And, by and large, that is what us mediums do: we offer hope to people, often when they are in desperate circumstances. We can offer hope to those who think there is no point in going on. We can offer positives when there only seem to be negatives. I believe that, in the last couple of decades, more and more people are realizing the value of what genuine mediums can offer. There is a spiritual drought afflicting us at the moment and a sense of hopelessness that pervades huge swathes of the population. It is very easy to lose sight of our spiritual selves in the twenty-first century.

Traditionally, religion fulfilled the role of keeping people in tune with their spirituality but, for various reasons, religion seems to be suffering a crisis of faith today, and this is at a time when people are probably more in need of a spiritual boost than they ever have been.

It's very easy to get worn down by all the negativity in the world. Sometimes you switch on the news and the doom and gloom can be overpowering. Bulletin after bulletin details death and disaster, recession and depression. People are worried about their jobs and their homes and the world their children are growing up in. They need hope and they need to know there is something more in life and, increasingly, they turn to mediums.

I've definitely noticed that there is more demand for mediums when times are tough. During the recession in the nineties, I had more enquiries than ever. Some were from businessmen hoping for insight and others from people worried about how they were going to pay their bills. I don't get spirit coming through with the winning lottery numbers or the name of the winner in the 3.45 at Sandown, but what I do get are messages of reassurance. Spirit comes through to say, 'Don't worry, it will work out in the end.'

And after 9/11 I noticed a spike in demand too. As a nation, we were so fearful of what was happening in the world people wanted reassurance, and what better reassurance can there be than the knowledge that, no matter how much we suffer in our lives here, no matter how hopeless life appears to be, there is something better awaiting us.

The ability to have such a profound effect on people's lives at such sensitive times is not something I take lightly, and it doesn't come without responsibility. I take that responsibility very seriously. I know I've been blessed with the ability I have and I know it is there for a reason. I know it is imperative that I stay faithful to the messages I receive and that I empathize with the people I give messages to. There are no gimmicks during my shows, and I don't use props. I remind myself of my shortcomings every day. It would be easy to get too big for my boots, but the moment that happens I know I'll lose the authenticity and the openness that spirits are attracted to. And if that happens, the ability goes. I try to remain as humble as possible about my work, and I use plain English. I try not to dress up what I do in mysticism and mumbo-jumbo because, as far as I am concerned, there's no mysticism about it: I talk to dead people.

I am a messenger. I haven't got all the answers. I probably never will have. I'm only just starting to understand the mechanics of this ability I have and how it functions. I'm only just starting to realize the importance of psychic energy and how it binds the living and the dead together. I know I was meant to be doing what I do and I know that it is my job to send out the message that there is an afterlife, that death is not the end. I was meant to give people hope, to give them evidence of the afterlife and to make them happy. For me, there is no bigger or better purpose than that.

No matter how desperate things appear, no matter how wrapped up and weighed down with grief you are, there is just one truth that you need to know, just one fact that will wash all the pain away. It's as simple as this: there *is* something else, there *is* an afterlife, and through it you will find love and peace.

Acknowledgements

In memory of my sister-in-law Jean, who sadly passed in March 2010.

Jean was an incredibly brave lady who battled MS for over twenty-five years. She will be deeply missed by all her family, but I take great comfort in the knowledge that she is now in Heaven and with her father.

Thank you Daniel Bunyard, Katy Follain and all the team at Penguin for your amazing support, and for giving me the opportunity to put into words my feelings and experiences.

Lastly, I want to thank my friend Nick Harding for all his help and guidance in putting this book together.

He just wanted a decent book to read ...

Not too much to ask, is it? It was in 1935 when Allen Lane, Managing Director of Bodley Head Publishers, stood on a platform at Exeter railway station looking for something good to read on his journey back to London. His choice was limited to popular magazines and poor-quality paperbacks – the same choice faced every day by the vast majority of readers, few of whom could afford hardbacks. Lane's disappointment and subsequent anger at the range of books generally available led him to found a company – and change the world.

'We believed in the existence in this country of a vast reading public for intelligent books at a low price, and staked everything on it'
Sir Allen Lane, 1902–1970, founder of Penguin Books

The quality paperback had arrived – and not just in bookshops. Lane was adamant that his Penguins should appear in chain stores and tobacconists, and should cost no more than a packet of cigarettes.

Reading habits (and cigarette prices) have changed since 1935, but Penguin still believes in publishing the best books for everybody to enjoy. We still believe that good design costs no more than bad design, and we still believe that quality books published passionately and responsibly make the world a better place.

So wherever you see the little bird – whether it's on a piece of prize-winning literary fiction or a celebrity autobiography, political tour de force or historical masterpiece, a serial-killer thriller, reference book, world classic or a piece of pure escapism – you can bet that it represents the very best that the genre has to offer.

Whatever you like to read – trust Penguin.